GROSSET'S

SPANISH

PHRASE BOOK
AND
DICTIONARY

by Charles A. Hughes

A GD/PERIGEE BOOK

D0250401

OTHER BOOKS IN THIS SERIES:

Grosset's French Phrase Book
and Dictionary for Travelers

•

Grosset's German Phrase Book
and Dictionary for Travelers

•

Grosset's Italian Phrase Book
and Dictionary for Travelers

Perigee Books
are published by
The Putnam Publishing Group
200 Madison Avenue
New York, New York 10016

LC: 73-144059
ISBN 0-399-50792-2

First Perigee printing, 1982
Printed in the United States of America

14   15   16   17   18   19   20

CONTENTS

Introduction........................ v
Tips on Pronunciation and Accent.... vi
Salutations and Greetings............ 1
The Weather....................... 5
General Expressions................ 9
Emergencies......................15
Signs and Notices..................18
Numbers, Time and Dates...........21
Changing Money...................31
Customs.........................34
At the Hotel......................37
Using the Telephone...............43
Getting Around by Taxi and Bus.....46
Eating and Drinking...............50
Menu Reader.....................60
Shopping........................64
Getting Around by Automobile......75
Getting Around by Train...........85
Getting Around by Ship and Plane....89
Health..........................94
Sightseeing......................100
Dictionary......................105

INTRODUCTION

In this phrase book for travel in Spanish-speaking countries, we have tried to incorporate features that will make it convenient and easy for you to use in actual situations. Every phrase and word is translated into proper Spanish and then respelled to guide you in its pronunciation.

The book is also "programmed" to help you with two of the basic problems of the novice in a language — an inability to comprehend the spoken word and a certain hesitancy in speaking out. To solve the first problem, questions have been avoided, to the extent possible, in the phrases. When they could not be avoided, they have been worded so that a yes or no answer may be expected. And sometimes, when even this solution is impossible, the anticipated answer is given. To solve the problem of hesitancy, the contents of the book have been arranged so that a minimal command of the basic phrases, salutations, weather, numbers, time, statements of need and desire, may be acquired in the first sections. The pronunciation guides printed under the Spanish translations should also give you confidence that you will be understood. If your listener should indicate that he doesn't understand, merely try again. A slight mispronunciation is no embarrassment.

Finally, to aid you in finding a phrase that you wish to use, the Dictionary has been partially indexed. The Dictionary itself is comprehensive enough so that you will not lack the basic words for any usual situation.

TIPS ON PRONUNCIATION AND ACCENT

The pronunciation of each word in this phrase book is indicated by a respelling that approximates the sounds of Spanish, according to the following system:

The vowels:

ah	Pronounced like "a" in f*a*ther
eh	Pronounced like "e" in m*e*n
ee	Pronounced like "ee" in s*ee*n
oh	Pronounced like "o" in *o*ver
oo	Pronounced like "oo" in s*oo*n
ah-ee	Pronounced like the pronoun *I* or the word *eye*
ow	Pronounced like "ow" in n*ow*
weh	Pronounced like "we" in *we*t
oy	Pronounced like "oy" in b*oy*

Consonants are sounded approximately as in English, with these exceptions:

"c" before "a," "o" and "u" sounds like the "c" in *c*an.

"c" before "e" and "i" sounds like the "c" in *c*ent in Latin America and like the "th" of *th*ink in Castillian Spanish.

"g" before "a," "o" and "u" sounds like the "g" in *g*o.

"g" before "e" and "i" sounds like the "h" in *h*orse, but with a little more vibration.

"h" is always silent.

"j" sounds like the "h" in *h*orse, but with a little more vibration.

"ll" sounds like the "ll" in mi*ll*ion.

"ñ" sounds like the "n" in ca*n*yon.

"r" is always slightly trilled.

"rr" is more strongly trilled.

"s" sounds like "s" in *s*in.

"z" sounds like "s" in *s*in in Latin America, but like "th" in *th*ink in Castillian Spanish.

In the pronunciations, the stress or main accent in a word is indicated by an accent mark (') after the stressed syllable.

heart	**four**
corazón	cuatro
koh-rah-sohn'	*kwah'-troh*

Salutations and Greetings

Even before you learn anything else in a foreign language, you will want to learn how to greet people. Here are some short expressions that you will find easy to learn and to use when you meet people in a foreign land or along the way, perhaps on the ship or the plane.

Good morning.
Buenos días.
Bweh'-nohs dee'-ahs.

Good day.
Buenos días.
Bweh'-nohs dee'-ahs.

Good afternoon.
Buenas tardes.
Bweh'-nahs tahr'-dehs.

Good evening.
Buenas noches.
Bweh'-nahs noh'-chehs.

Good-bye.
Adiós.
Ah-dee-ohs'.

Good-night.
Buenas noches.
Bweh'-nahs noh'-chehs.

How are you?
¿Cómo está usted?
Koh'-moh eh-stah' oos-tehd'?

Well, thank you. And you?
Bien, gracias. ¿Y usted?
Byehn grah'-syahs. Ee oos-tehd'?

How is Mr. . . . ?
¿Cómo está el señor . . . ?
Koh'-moh eh-stah' ehl seh-nyohr' . . . ?

How is Mrs. . . . ?
¿Cómo está la señora . . . ?
Koh'-moh eh-stah' lah seh-nyoh'-rah . . . ?

Is Miss . . . well?
¿Está bien la señorita . . . ?
Eh-stah' byehn lah seh-nyoh-ree'-tah . . .?

May I present my wife?
¿Puedo presentar a mi esposa?
Pweh'-doh preh-sehn-tahr' ah mee eh-spoh'-sah?

This is my husband.
Éste es mi esposo (marido).
Eh'-steh ehs mee eh-spoh'-soh (mah-ree'-doh).

Pleased to meet you.
Mucho gusto en conocerle.
Moo'-choh goo'-stoh ehn koh-noh-sehr'-leh.

This is my friend.
Éste es mi amigo (m).
Eh'-steh ehs mee ah-mee'-goh.

This is my friend.
Ésta es mi amiga (f).
Eh'-stah ehs mee ah-mee'-gah.

This is my mother and my father.
Ésta es mi madre y éste es mi padre.
Eh'-stah ehs mee mah'-dreh ee eh'-steh ehs mee pah'-dreh.

This is my sister and my brother.
Ésta es mi hermana y éste es mi hermano.
Eh'-stah ehs mee ehr-mah'-nah ee eh'-steh ehs mee ehr-mah'-noh.

Is this your daughter?
¿ Es ésta su hija?
Ehs eh'-stah soo ee'-hah?

Is this your son?
¿ Es éste su hijo?
Ehs eh-steh soo ee'-hoh?

I hope that we will meet again.
Espero que nos encontremos otra vez.
Eh-speh-roh keh nohs ehn-kohn-treh'-mohs oh'-trah vehs.

I'll see you tomorrow.
Hasta mañana.
Ah'-stah mah-nyah'-nah.

I'll be seeing you.
Hasta luego. / Hasta la vista.
Ah'-stah lweh'-goh. / Ah'-stah lah vee'-stah.

Excuse me.
Dispénseme.
Dee-spehn'-seh-meh.

Pardon me.
Perdone.
Pehr-doh'-neh.

I'm very sorry.
Lo siento mucho.
Loh syehn'-toh moo'-choh.

Don't mention it.
No hay de qué. / De nada.
Noh ah'-ee deh keh. / Deh nah'-dah.

You're welcome.
De nada. / No hay de qué.
Deh nah'-dah. / Noh ah'-ee deh keh.

With pleasure.
Con mucho gusto.
Kohn moo'-choh goo'-stoh.

Please.
Por favor.
Pohr fah-vohr'.

Please . . .
Sírvase . . .
Seer'-vah-seh . . .

Good luck!
¡Buena suerte!
Bweh'-nah swehr'-teh!

The Weather

The weather is one thing everyone has in common, and it is a universal topic of conversation. The phrases given here — combined with a bit of added vocabulary — are easily mastered, for they "pattern" in an understandable manner: "It's raining." "It's snowing."

It's nice weather today.
Hoy hace buen tiempo.
Oy ah'-seh bwehn tyehm'-poh.

It's bad weather today.
Hoy hace mal tiempo.
Oy ah'-seh mahl tyehm'-poh.

It's cold.
Hace frío.
Ah'-seh free'-yoh.

It's warm.
Hace calor.
Ah'-seh kah-lohr'.

Is it raining?
¿Está lloviendo?
Eh-stah' lyoh-vyehn'-doh?

Yes, it's raining.
Sí, está lloviendo.
See eh-stah' lyoh-vyehn'-doh.

No, it's not raining.
No, no está lloviendo.
Noh noh eh-stah'
lyoh-vyehn'-doh.

It's snowing.
Está nevando.
Eh-stah' neh-vahn'-doh.

It rains (snows) here every day.
Aquí llueve (nieva) todos los días.
Ah-kee' lyweh'-veh (nyeh'-vah) toh'-dohs lohs dee'-ahs.

It's beginning to rain (to snow).
Empieza a llover (nevar).
Ehm-pyeh'-sah ah lyoh-vehr' (neh-vahr').

It often rains (snows) here.
Aquí llueve (nieva) a menudo.
Ah-kee' lyweh'-veh (nyeh'-vah) ah meh-noo'-doh.

It will rain (snow) tomorrow.
Mañana lloverá (nevará).
Mah-nyah'-nah lyoh-veh-rah' (neh-vah-rah').

It rained (snowed) yesterday.
Ayer llovió (nevó).
Ah-yehr' lyoh-vyoh' (neh-voh').

It has stopped raining (snowing).
Ha cesado de llover (nevar).
Ah seh-sah'-doh deh lyoh-vehr' (neh-vahr').

It's windy.
Hace viento.
Ah'-seh vyehn'-toh.

There's a lot of fog.
Hay mucha niebla.
Ah'-ee moo'-chah nyeh'-blah.

The sun is rising.
El sol se levanta.
Ehl sohl seh leh-vahn'-tah.

The sun is setting.
El sol se pone.
Ehl sohl seh poh'-neh.

I see . . .
Veo . . .
Veh'-yoh . . .

I like . . .
Me gusta(n) . . .
Meh goos'-tah(n) . . .

I'm afraid of . . .
Tengo miedo de . . .
Tehn'-goh myehd'-doh deh . . .

the rain.
la lluvia.
lah lyoo'-vyah.

the wind.
el viento.
ehl vyehn'-toh.

the ice.
el hielo.
ehl yeh'-loh.

the sky.
el cielo.
ehl syeh'-loh.

the snow.
la nieve.
lah nyeh'-veh.

the sun.
el sol.
ehl sohl.

the moon.
la luna.
lah loo'-nah.

the stars.
las estrellas.
lahs eh-streh'-lyahs.

a rainbow.
un arco iris.
oon ahr'-koh ee'-rees.

a cloud.
una nube.
oo'-nah noo'-beh

the lightning.
el relámpago.
ehl reh-lahm'-pah-goh.

the thunder.
el trueno.
ehl trweh'-noh.

a star.
una estrella.
oo'-nah eh-streh'-lyah.

the clouds.
las nubes.
lahs noo'-behs.

the storm.
la tempestad.
lah tehm-pehs-tahd'.

How is the weather?
¿Qué tiempo hace?
Keh tyehm'-poh ah'-seh?

I need an umbrella.
Necesito un paraguas.
Neh-seh-see'-toh oon pah-rah'-gwahs.

Will it be cool there?
¿Hará tiempo fresco allá?
Ah-rah' tyehm'-poh frehs'-koh ah-lyah'?

Will it be damp there?
¿Hará tiempo húmedo allá?
Ah-rah' tyehm'-poh hoo'-meh-doh ah-lyah'?

Should I take a sweater?
¿Debería llevar un suéter?
Deh-beh-ree'-yah lyeh-yahr' oon sweh'-tehr?

a raincoat?
un impermeable?
oon eem-pehr-meh-ah'-bleh?

a jacket?
una chaqueta?
oo'-nah chah-keh'-tah?

It's lightning.
Hay relámpago.
Ah'-ee reh-lahm'-pah-goh.

It's thundering.
Truena.
Trweh'-nah.

Cold weather.
Tiempo frío.
Tyehm'-poh free'-yoh.

Warm weather.
Tiempo caliente.
Tyehm'-poh kahl-yehn'-teh.

Cold water.
Agua fría.
Ah'-gwah free'-yah.

Warm water.
Agua caliente.
Ah'-gwah kahl-yehn'-teh.

Hot water.
Agua muy caliente.
Ah'-gwah mwee kahl-yehn'-teh.

General Expressions

In this section you will find the most useful expressions — the ones you will use over and over again. They are the phrases that you should have on the tip of the tongue, ready for immediate use — particularly those that express desire or volition. Here they have been kept short for easy acquisition and speedy communication. You will see them appear again and again in other sections of this book, where they are used in particular situations.

What is your name?
¿Cómo se llama usted?
*Koh'-moh seh lyah'-mah
oos-tehd'?*

My name is . . .
Me llamo . . .
Meh lyah'-moh . . .

What is his (her) name?
¿Cómo se llama?
Koh'-moh seh lyah'-mah?

I don't know.
No sé.
Noh seh.

His (Her) name is . . .
Él (Ella) se llama . . .
Ehl (Ehl'-yah) seh lyah'-mah . . .

Do you know him (her)?
¿Lo (La) conoce usted?
*Loh (Lah) koh-noh'-seh
oos-tehd'?*

Yes, I know him (her).
Sí, lo (la) conozco.
*See loh (lah)
koh-nohs'-koh.*

No, I don't know him (her).
No, no lo (la) conozco.
*Noh loh (lah)
koh-nohs'-koh.*

I know you.
Le conozco a usted.
*Leh koh-nohs'-koh
ah oos-tehd'.*

Where do you live?
?Dónde vive usted?
*Dohn'-deh vee'-veh
oos-tehd'?*

I live here.
Vivo aquí.
Vee'-voh ah-kee'.

At which hotel are you staying?
¿En qué hotel se hospeda usted?
Ehn keh oh'-tehl' seh ohs-peh'-dah oos-tehd'?

She's a beautiful woman.
Es una mujer hermosa.
*Ehs oo'-nah moo-hehr'
ehr-moh'-sah.*

She's a pretty girl.
Es una muchacha bonita.
*Ehs oo'-nah moo-chah'-
chah boh-nee'tah.*

He's a handsome man.
Es un hombre guapo.
*Ehs oon ohm'-breh
gwah'-poh.*

I love her.
La quiero. La amo.
*Lah kyeh'-roh.
Lah ah'-moh.*

I love you.
Te quiero. Te amo.
Teh kyeh'-roh. Teh ah'-moh.

I love him.
Lo quiero. Lo amo.
Loh kyeh'-roh.Loh ah'-moh.

Do you know where he lives?
¿Sabe usted dónde vive?
Sah'-beh oos-tehd' dohn'-deh vee'-veh?

Do you speak English?
¿Habla usted inglés?
Ah'-blah oos-tehd' een-glehs'?

Please say it in English.
Dígalo en inglés, por favor.
Dee'-gah-loh ehn een-glehs', pohr fah-vohr'.

Is there anyone here who speaks English?
¿Hay alguien aquí que hable inglés?
Ah'-ee ahl'-gyehn ah-kee' keh ah'-bleh een-glehs'?

Do you understand?
¿Entiende usted? ¿Comprende usted?
Ehn-tyehn'-deh oos-tehd'? Kohm-prehn'-deh oos-tehd'?

Yes, I understand.
Sí, entiendo. Sí, comprendo.
See ehn-tyehn'-doh. See kohm-prehn'-doh.

No, I don't understand.
No, no entiendo (comprendo).
Noh, noh ehn-tyehn'-doh (kohm-prehn'-doh).

I understand a little.
Entiendo (Comprendo) un poco.
Ehn-tyehn'-doh (kohm-prehn'-doh) oon poh'-koh.

I don't understand everything.
No entiendo (comprendo) todo.
Noh ehn-tyehn'-doh (kohm-prehn'-doh) toh'do h).

Please speak more slowly.
Hable más despacio, por favor.
Ah'-bleh mahs dehs-pah'-syoh, pohr fah-vohr'.

Please repeat.
Repita, por favor.
Reh-pee'-tah, pohr fah-vohr'.

What did you say?
¿Qué dijo usted?
Keh dee'-hoh oos-tehd'?

How do you say that in Spanish?
¿Cómo se dice eso en español?
Koh'-moh seh dee'-seh eh'-soh, ehn eh-spah-nyohl'?

What does that mean?
¿Qué significa eso?
Keh seeg-nee-fee'-kah eh'-soh?

What do you mean?
¿Qué quiere usted decir?
Keh kyeh'-reh oos-tehd' deh-seer'?

You are right.
Usted tiene razón.
Oos-tehd' tyeh'-neh rah-sohn'.

He is right.
Él tiene razón.
Ehl tyeh'-neh rah-sohn'.

You are wrong.
No tiene razón.
Noh tyeh'-neh rah-sohn'.

He is wrong.
No tiene razón.
Noh tyeh'-neh rah-sohn'.

Without doubt.
Sin duda.
Seen doo'-dah.

Where are you going?
¿Adónde va usted?
Ah-dohn'-deh vah oos-tehd'?

Where is he going?
¿Adónde va él?
Ah-dohn'-deh vah ehl?

Where are we going?
¿Adónde vamos?
Ah-dohn'-deh vah'-mohs?

I will wait here.
Esperaré aquí.
Eh-speh-rah-reh' ah-kee'.

How long must I wait?
¿Cuánto tiempo tengo que esperar?
Kwahn'-toh tyehm'-poh tehn'-goh keh eh-speh-rahr'?

Wait here until I come back.
Espere aquí hasta que vuelva.
Eh-speh'-reh ah-kee' ahs'-tah keh vwehl'-vah.

Bring me . . .
Tráigame . . .
Trah'-ee-gah-meh . .

Tell me . . .
Dígame . . .
Dee'-gah-meh . . .

Give me . . .
Déme . . .
Deh'-meh . . .

Show me . . .
Muéstreme . . .
Mweh'-streh-meh . . .

Send me . . .
Mándeme (Envíeme) . . .
*Mahn'-deh-meh
(Ehn-vee'-eh-meh) . . .*

Write to me . . .
Escríbame . . .
Eh-skree'-bah-meh . . .

I need . . .
Necesito . . .
Neh-seh-see'-toh . . .

I would like . . .
Quisiera (Desearía) . . .
*Kee-syeh'-rah (Deh-seh-
ah-ree'-yah) . . .*

I want . . .
Quiero (Deseo) . . .
Kyeh'-roh (Deh-seh'-oh) . . .

I don't want . . .
No quiero (deseo) . .
*Noh kyeh'-roh
(deh-seh'-oh) . . .*

I can do that.
Puedo hacer eso.
Pweh'-doh ah-sehr' eh'-soh.

I cannot do that.
No puedo hacer eso.
*Noh pweh'-doh ah-sehr'
eh'-soh.*

Have you . . . ?
¿Tiene usted . . . ?
Tyeh'-neh oos-tehd' . . . ?

Are you . . . ?
¿Es usted . . . ? ¿Está usted . . . ?
Ehs oos-tehd' . . . ? Eh-stah' oos-tehd' . . . ?

Where is . . . ?
¿Dónde está . . . ?
Dohn'-deh eh-stah' . . . ?

Where are . . . ?
¿Dónde están . . . ?
Dohn'-deh eh-stahn' . . . ?

Come here.
Venga acá.
Vehn'-gah ah-kah'.

Come in.
Entre.
Ehn'-treh.

It's possible.
Es posible.
Ehs poh-see'-bleh.

Is it near here?
¿Está cerca de aquí?
*Eh-stah' sehr'-kah
deh ah-kee'?*

Is it far from here?
¿Está lejos de aquí?
*Eh-stah' leh'-hohs deh
ah-kee'?*

It's impossible.
Es imposible.
Ehs eem-poh-see'-bleh.

Emergencies

You will probably never need to use any of the brief cries, entreaties, or commands that appear here, but accidents do happen, items may be mislaid or stolen, and mistakes do occur. If an emergency does arise, it will probably be covered by one of these expressions.

Help!
¡Socorro!
Soh-koh'-rroh!

Help me!
¡Ayúdeme!
Ah-yoo'-deh-meh!

There has been an accident!
¡Ha sucedido un accidente!
Ah soo-seh-dee'-doh oon ahk-see-dehn'-teh!

Stop!
¡Pare!
Pah'-reh!

Hurry up!
¡De prisa!
Deh pree'-sah!

Look out!
¡Cuidado!
Kwee-dah'-doh!

Send for a doctor!
¡Mande venir un médico!
Mahn'-deh veh-neer' oon meh'-dee-koh!

Poison!
¡Veneno!
Veh-neh'-noh!

Fire!
¡Incendio!
Een-sehn'-dee-oh

Police!
¡Policía!
Poh-lee-see'-yah!

What happened?
¿Qué pasó?
Keh pah-soh'?

What's the matter?
¿Qué hay?
Keh ah'-ee?

Don't worry!
!No se preocupe!
Noh seh preh-oh-koo'-peh!

I've been robbed!
¡Me han robado!
Meh ahn roh-bah'-doh!

I missed the train (bus) (plane)!
¡He perdido el tren (autobús) (avión)!
Eh pehr-dee'-doh ehl trehn (ow-toh-boos') (ah-vyohn')!

That man stole my money!
¡Ese hombre me robó el dinero!
Eh'-seh ohm'-breh meh roh-boh' ehl dee-neh'-roh!

Call the police!
¡Llame a la policía!
Lyah'-meh ah lah poh-lee-see'-yah!

I have lost my money.
He perdido mi dinero.
Eh pehr-dee'-doh mee dee-neh'-roh.

I have lost my passport!
¡He perdido mi pasaporte!
Eh pehr-dee'-doh mee pah-sah-pohr'-teh!

It's an American (British) passport.
Es un pasaporte americano (inglés).
Ehs oon pah-sah-pohr'-teh ah-meh-ree-kah'-noh(een-glehs').

Stay where you are!
¡Quédese donde está!
*Keh'-deh-seh dohn'-deh
  eh-stah'!*

Don't move!
¡No se mueva!
Noh seh mweh'-vah!

Signs and Notices

You could probably get along in a foreign land without speaking a word if only you could read the signs and notices posted and displayed as directions and advertising. A sign is an immediate communication to him who can read it, and the pronunciation doesn't matter. To help you in some usual situations, here are the common signs. Some of them will help you avoid embarrassment, and others danger. And some of them will merely make life more pleasant.

ABIERTO, Open
ADELANTE, Go
A LA DERECHA, To the right
A LA IZQUIERDA, To the left
ALARMA DE INCENDIOS, Fire alarm
AVISO, Warning
BAÑO, Bathroom

CABALLEROS, Men
CAJA, Cashier
CALIENTE, Warm
CAMINO ESTRECHO, Narrow road
CERRADO, Closed
COLINA, Hill
COMEDOR, Dining room
CRUCE DE TRENES, Railroad crossing
CUIDADO, Caution
CURVA, Curve
CURVA PELIGROSA, Dangerous curve
DAMAS, Women
DESPACIO, Slow
DESVÍO, Detour
DIRECCIÓN ÚNICA, One way
EMPUJE, Push
ENCRUCIJADA PELIGROSA, Dangerous crossroad
ENTRADA, Entrance
ENTRADA LIBRE, Admission free
ESCUELA, School
ES PELIGROSO, It's dangerous
ESPERE, Wait
ESTACIONAMIENTO, Parking
ECXUSADO, Toilet
FRÍO, Cold
GUARDE SU DERECHA, Keep to the right
HOMBRES, Men
IGLESIA, Church
INFORMES, Information
LAVABOS, Lavatory
LIBRE, Free
MUJERES, Women
MANEJE DESPACIO, Go slow
NO FUME, No smoking
NO HAY PASAJE, No thoroughfare
NO TOME EL AGUA, Do not drink the water

NO TOQUE, Do not touch
NO VUELVA A LA DERECHA, No right turn
NO VUELVA A LA IZQUIERDA, No left turn
OCUPADO, Occupied
PARE, Stop
PELIGRO, Danger
PROHIBIDO, Forbidden
PUENTE ESTRECHO, Narrow bridge
RETRETE, Toilet
SALA DE ESPERA, Waiting room
SALIDA, Exit
SE ALQUILAN HABITACIONES AMUEBLADAS,
  Furnished rooms to let
SE PERMITE FUMAR, Smoking allowed
SE PROHIBE ENTRAR, Do not enter
SE PROHIBE ESTACIONAR, No parking
SE PROHIBE FUMAR, No smoking
TIRE, Pull
TOALLAS, Hand towels
TOQUE, Ring
TRÁNSITO, One way

Numbers, Time and Dates

You may only want to count your change or make an appointment or catch a train, but you will need to know the essentials of counting and telling time if you wish to stay on schedule, buy gifts, or pay for accommodations. In Europe, you should remember, time is told by a twenty-four hour system. Thus 10 P.M., in Spain, is 2200 and 10:30 P.M. is 2230.

Cardinal Numbers

one	**two**
un, uno, una	dos
oon, oo′-noh, oo′-nah	*dohs*
three	**four**
tres	cuatro
trehs	*kawh′-troh*
five	**six**
cinco	seis
seen′-koh	*seh′-ees*

seven
siete
syeh'-teh

eight
ocho
oh'-choh

nine
nueve
nweh'-veh

ten
diez
dyehs

eleven
once
ohn'-seh

twelve
doce
doh'-seh

thirteen
trece
treh'-seh

fourteen
catorce
kah-tohr'-seh

fifteen
quince
keen'-seh

sixteen
dieciséis
dyehs-ee-seh'-ees

seventeen
diecisiete
dyehs-ee-syeh'-teh

eighteen
dieciocho
dyehs-ee-oh'-choh

nineteen
diecinueve
dyehs-ee-nweh'-veh

twenty
veinte
veh'-een-teh

twenty-one
veintiuno
veh-een-tee-oo'-noh

twenty-two
veintidós
veh-een-tee-dohs'

thirty
treinta
treh'-een-tah

thirty-one
treinta y uno
treh'-een-tah ee oo'-noh

forty
cuarenta
kwah-rehn'-tah

fifty
cincuenta
seen-kwehn'-tah

sixty
sesenta
seh-sehn'-tah

seventy
setenta
seh-tehn'-tah

eighty
ochenta
oh-chehn'-tah

ninety
noventa
noh-vehn'-tah

one hundred
ciento, cien
syehn'-toh, syehn

two hundred
doscientos
dohs-syehn'-tohs

three hundred
trescientos
trehs-syehn'-tohs

five hundred
quinientos
kee-nyehn'-tohs

one thousand
mil
meel

one million
un millón
oon mee-lyohn'

nineteen hundred seventy . . .
mil novecientos setenta . . .
meel noh-veh-syehn'-tohs seh-tehn'-tah

one man
un hombre
oon ohm'-breh

one woman
una mujer
oo'-nah moo-hehr'

one child
un niño
oon nee'-nyoh

two men
dos hombres
dohs ohm'-brehs

two women
dos mujeres
dohs moo-hehr'-ehs

two children
dos niños
dos nee'-nyohs

Some Ordinal Numbers

the first
el primero
ehl pree-meh'-roh

the second
el segundo
ehl seh-goon'-doh

the third
el tercero
ehl tehr-seh'-roh

the fourth
el cuarto
ehl kwahr'-toh

the fifth
el quinto
ehl keen'-toh

the sixth
el sexto
ehl sehk'-stoh

the seventh
el séptimo
ehl sehp'-tee-moh

the eighth
el octavo
ehl ohk-tah'-voh

the ninth
el noveno
ehl noh-veh'-noh

the tenth
el décimo
ehl deh'-see-moh

the first man
el primer hombre
ehl pree-mehr' ohm'-breh

the first woman
la primera mujer
lah pree-meh'-rah moo-hehr'

the first child
el primer niño
ehl pree-mehr' nee'-nyoh

the third day
el tercer día
ehl tehr-sehr' dee'-ah

the fourth street
la cuarta calle
lah kwahr'-tah kah'-lyeh

the fifth floor
el quinto piso
ehl keen'-toh pee'-soh

the second building
el segundo edificio
ehl seh-goon'-doh eh-dee-fee'-syoh

Telling Time

What time is it?
¿Qué hora es?
Keh oh'-rah ehs?

It's two o'clock
Son las dos.
Sohn lahs dohs.

It's half-past two.
Son las dos y media.
Sohn lahs dohs ee meh'-dee-yah.

It's ten after two.
Son las dos y diez.
Sohn lahs dohs ee dyehs.

It's five o'clock.
Son las cinco.
Sohn lahs seen'-koh.

It's noon.
Es mediodía.
Ehs meh-dee-yoh-dee'-yah.

It's early.
Es temprano.
Ehs tehm-prah'-noh.

one second
un segundo
oon seh-goon'-doh

It's one o'clock.
Es la una.
Ehs lah oo'-nah.

It's a quarter after two.
Son las dos y cuarto.
Sohn lahs dohs ee kwahr'-toh.

It's a quarter till two.
Son las dos menos cuarto.
Sohn lahs dohs meh'-nohs kwahr'-toh.

It's ten till two.
Son las dos menos diez.
Sohn lahs dohs meh'-nohs dyehs.

It's ten o'clock.
Son las diez.
Sohn lahs dyehs.

It's midnight.
Es medianoche.
Ehs meh-dee-yah-noh'-cheh.

It's late.
Es tarde.
Ehs tahr'-deh.

five seconds
cinco segundos
seen'-koh seh-goon'-dohs

one minute
un minuto
oon mee-noo'-toh

five minutes
cinco minutos
seen'-koh mee-noo'-tohs

one quarter hour
un cuarto de hora
oon kwahr'-toh deh oh'-rah

one half hour
una media hora
oo'-nah meh'-dee-yah oh'-rah

one hour
una hora
oo'-nah oh'-rah

five hours
cinco horas
seen'-koh oh'-rahs

At what time are you leaving?
¿A qué hora sale usted?
Ah keh oh'-rah sah'-leh oos-tehd'?

When do you arrive?
¿Cuándo llega usted?
Kwahn'-doh lyeh'-gah oos-tehd'?

When will we arrive?
¿Cuándo llegaremos?
Kwahn'-doh lyeh-gah-reh'-mohs?

When shall we meet?
¿Cuándo nos encontraremos?
Kwahn'-doh nohs ehn-kohn-trah-reh'-mohs?

Meet me here at five o'clock.
Encuéntreme aquí a las cinco.
Ehn-kwehn'-treh-meh ah-kee' ah lahs seen'-koh.

At what time do you get up?
¿A qué hora se levanta usted?
Ah keh oh'-rah seh leh-vahn'-tah oos-tehd'?

At what time do you go to bed?
¿A qué hora se acuesta usted?
Ah keh oh'-rah seh ah-kwehs'-tah?

Dates

today
hoy
oy

tomorrow
mañana
mah-nyah'-nah

yesterday
ayer
ah-yehr'

one day
un día
oon dee'-yah

two days
dos días
dohs dee'-yahs

five days
cinco días
seen'-koh dee'-yahs

the day after tomorrow
pasado mañana
pah-sah'-doh mah-nyah'-nah

the day before yesterday
anteayer
ahn-teh-ăh-yehr'

the morning
la mañana
lah mah-nyah'-nah

the afternoon
la tarde
lah tahr'-deh

the evening
la noche
lah noh'-cheh

the night
la noche
lah noh'-cheh

the week
la semana
lah seh-mah'-nah

the month
el mes
ehl mehs

the year
el año
ehl ah'-nyoh

last week
la semana pasada
lah seh-mah'-nah pah-sah'-dah

last month
el mes pasado
ehl mehs pah-sah'-doh

last year
el año pasado
ehl ah'-nyoh pah-sah'-doh

this week
esta semana
eh'-stah seh-mah'-nah

this month
este mes
eh'-steh mehs

this year
este año
eh'-steh ah'-nyoh

next week
la semana próxima
lah seh-mah'-nah prok'-see-mah

next month
el mes próximo
hle mehs prok'-see-moh

next year
el año próximo
ehl ah'-nyoh prok'-see-moh

this morning
esta mañana
eh'-stah mah-nyah'-nah

yesterday morning
ayer por la mañana
ah-yehr' pohr lah mah-nyah'-nah

tomorrow morning
mañana por la mañana
mah-nyah'-nah pohr lah mah-nyah'-nah

this evening
esta noche
eh'-stah noh'-cheh

yesterday evening
ayer por la noche
ah-yehr' pohr lah noh'-cheh

tomorrow evening
mañana por la noche
mah-nyah'-nah pohr lah noh'-cheh

every day
todos los días
toh'-dohs lohs dee'-yahs

two days ago
hace dos días
ah'-seh dohs dee'-yahs

What day is today?
¿Qué día es hoy?
Keh dee'-yah ehs oy?

Today is the sixth.
Hoy es seis.
Oy ehs seh'-ees.

Yesterday was Monday.
Ayer fué lunes.
Ah-yehr' fweh loo'-nehs.

Tomorrow will be the seventh.
Mañana será siete.
Mah-nyah'-nah seh'-rah syeh'-teh.

The Days of the Week

Monday
lunes
loo'-nehs

Tuesday
martes
mahr'-tehs

Wednesday
miércoles
myehr'-koh-lehs

Thursday
jueves
hweh'-vehs

Friday
viernes
vyehr'-nehs

Saturday
sábado
sah'-bah-doh

Sunday
domingo
doh-meen'-goh

The Months of the Year

January
enero
eh-neh'-roh

February
febrero
feh-breh'-roh

March
marzo
mahr'-soh

April
abril
ah-breel'

May
mayo
mah'-yoh

June
junio
hoo'-nyoh

July
julio
hoo'-lyoh

August
agosto
ah-goh'-stoh

September
septiembre
sehp-tyehm'-breh

October
octubre
ohk-too'-breh

November
noviembre
noh-vyehm'-breh

December
diciembre
dee-syehm'-breh

The Seasons

the spring
la primavera
lah pree-mah-veh'-rah

the summer
el verano
ehl veh-rah'-noh

the autumn
el otoño
ehl oh-toh'-nyoh

the winter
el invierno
ehl een-vyehr'-noh

Changing Money

Whether poet or businessman, you will need cash as you travel. Sooner or later, every traveler meets the problem of how to manage the exchange. The following phrases cover most situations you will encounter. You will help yourself if you obtain the latest official exchange rate before you leave home, and it can do no harm if you familiarize yourself with the sizes, shapes, and even colors of the various coins and bills. It is wise, too, to take along a small amount of the foreign currency for immediate use on your arrival.

Where is the nearest bank?
¿Dónde está el banco más próximo?
Dohn'-deh eh-stah' ehl bahn'-koh mahs prohk'-see-moh?

Please write the address.
Escriba la dirección, por favor.
Eh-skree'-bah lah dee-rehk-syohn', pohr fah-vohr'.

I would like to cash this check.
Desearía cambiarme este cheque.
Deh-seh-ah-ree'-yah kahm-byahr'-meh es'-steh cheh'-keh.

Will you cash this check?
¿Me cambiará usted este cheque?
Meh kahm-byah-rah' oos-tehd' es'-steh cheh'-keh?

Do you accept travelers' checks?
¿Acepta usted cheques de viaje?
Ah-sehp'-tah oos-tehd' cheh'-kehs deh vyah'-heh?

I want to change some money.
Quiero cambiar dinero.
Kyeh'-roh kahm-byahr' dee-neh'-roh.

What kind?
¿Qué especie?
Keh eh-speh'-syeh?

Dollars.	**Pounds.**
Dólares.	Libras.
Doh'-lah-rehs.	*Lee'-brahs.*

What is the rate of exchange for the dollar (pound)?
¿Cómo está el cambio del dólar (de la libra)?
Koh'-moh eh-stah' ehl kahm'-byoh dehl doh'-lahr (deh lah lee'-brah)?

Your passport, please.
Su pasaporte, por favor.
Soo pah-sah-pohr'-teh, pohr fah-vohr.

How much do you wish to change?
¿Cuánto quiere usted cambiar?
Kwahn'-toh kyeh'-reh oos-tehd' kahm-byahr'?

I want to change ten dollars.
Quiero cambiar diez dólares.
Kyeh'-roh kahm-byahr' dyehs doh'-lah-rehs.

Go to that clerk's window.
Vaya a la ventanilla de ese empleado.
Vah'-yah ah lah vehn-tah-neel'-yah deh eh'-seh ehm-pleh-ah'-doh.

Here's the money.
He aquí el dinero.
Eh ah-kee' ehl dee-neh'-roh.

Here's your change.
He aquí su suelto.
Eh ah-kee' soo swehl'-toh.

Please give me some small change.
Sírvase darme menudo.
Seer'-vah-seh dahr'-meh meh-noo'-doh.

Please count to see if it's right.
Sírvase contarlo para determinar si es correcto.
Seer'-vah-seh kohn-tahr'-loh pah'-rah deh-tehr-mee-nahr' see ehs koh-rrehk'-toh.

Please sign this receipt.
Firme este recibo, por favor.
Feer'-meh eh'-steh reh-see'-boh, pohr fah-vohr'.

Can I change money here at the hotel?
¿Puedo cambiar dinero aquí en el hotel?
Pweh'-doh kahm-byahr' dee-neh'-roh ah-kee' ehn ehl oh-tehl'?

I'm expecting some money by mail.
Estoy esperando dinero por el correo.
Eh-stoy' eh-speh-rahn'-doh dee-neh'-roh pohr ehl koh-rreh'-oh.

Customs

Your first experience with Spanish may be with the personnel or fellow passengers on a ship or a plane, but you will really begin to use the language when you come to customs. Here are some phrases that will speed your entry into the country and get you on your way again.

Have you anything to declare?
¿Tiene usted algo que declarer?
Tyeh'-neh oos-tehd' ahl'-goh keh deh-klah-rahr'?

I have nothing to declare.
No tengo nada que declarar.
Noh tehn'-goh nah'-dah keh deh-klah-rahr'.

Your passport, please.
Su pasaporte, por favor.
Soo pah-sah-pohr'-teh, pohr fah-vohr'.

Here is my passport.
Aquí está mi pasaporte.
Ah-kee' eh-stah' mee pah-sah-pohr'-teh.

Are these your bags?
¿Son éstas sus maletas?
Sohn eh'-stahs soos mah-leh'-tahs?

Yes, and here are the keys.
Sí, y aquí están las llaves.
See, ee ah-kee' eh-stahn' lahs lyah'-vehs.

Open this box.
Abra esta caja.
Ah'-brah eh'-stah kah'-hah.

They are for my personal use.
Son para mi uso personal.
Sohn pah'-rah mee oo'-soh pehr-soh-nahl'.

Have you any cigarettes or tobacco?
¿Tiene usted cigarrillos o tabaco?
Tyeh'-neh oos-tehd' see-gah-rree'-lyohs oh tah-bah'-koh?

I have only some cigarettes.
Tengo sólo unos cigarrillos.
Tehn'-goh soh'-loh oo'-nohs see-gah-rree'-lyohs.

Close your bags.
Cierre sus sacos (maletas).
Syeh'-rreh soos sah'-kohs (mah-leh'-tahs).

You must pay duty.
Usted tiene que pagar derechos de aduana.
Oos-tehd' tyeh'-neh keh pah-gahr' deh-reh'-chohs deh ah-doo-ah'-nah.

How much must I pay?
¿Cuánto tengo que pagar?
Kwahn'-toh tehn'-goh keh
  pah-gahr'?

You must pay . . .
Usted tiene que pagar . . .
Oos-tehd' tyeh'-neh keh
  pah-gahr' . . .

May I go now?
¿Puedo ir ahora?
Pweh'-doh eer ah-oh'-rah?

Is that all?
¿Es eso todo?
Ehs eh'-soh toh'-doh?

Porter, please carry this luggage.
Mozo (Portero), lleve este equipaje, por favor.
Moh'-soh (pohr-teh'-roh), lyeh'-veh eh'-steh eh-kee-pah'-
  heh, pohr fah-vohr'.

At the Hotel

Your accommodations may be a deluxe hotel, a modest hotel, a pension, or whatever, but it is important to be able to express your needs to be sure you get what you want. Outside of the cities, of course, few people are likely to be able to help you if you do not speak Spanish, so we have given you the most useful expressions to cover most situations. They may make the difference between getting the room you want and having to settle for something less.

Which is the best hotel?
¿Cuál es el mejor hotel?
Kwahl ehs ehl meh-hohr'
  oh-tehl'?

I like this hotel.
Me gusta este hotel.
Meh goo'-stah eh'-steh oh-tehl'.

This is a good hotel.
Éste es un buen hotel.
Eh'-steh ehs oon bwehn oh-tehl'.

I would like to have a room here.
Quisiera hospedarme aquí.
Kee-syeh'-rah ohs-peh-dahr'-meh ah-kee'.

A single room.
Un cuarto para una persona.
Oon kwahr'-toh pah'-rah oo'-nah pehr-soh'-nah.

A double room.
Un cuarto para dos personas.
Oon kwahr'-toh pah'-rah dohs pehr-soh'-nahs.

A room with (without) bath.   **Is there a shower?**
Un cuarto con (sin) baño.   ¿Hay una ducha?
Oon kwahr'-toh kohn (seen)   Ah'-ee oo'-nah doo'-chah?
  bah'-nyoh.

May I see the room?
¿Puedo ver la habitación?
Pweh'-doh vehr lah ah-bee-tah-syohn'?

This is a large room.
Ésta es una habitación grande.
Eh'-stah ehs oo'-nah ah-bee-tah-syohn' grahn'-deh.

This room is too small.
Esta habitación es demasiado pequeña.
*Eh-stah ah-bee-tah-syohn' ehs deh-mah-syah'-doh
  peh-keh'-nyah.*

The room faces the street.
La habitación da a la calle.
Lah ah-bee-tah-syohn' dah ah lah kah'-lyeh.

Do you have a quieter room?
¿Tiene una habitación más silenciosa?
*Tyeh'-neh oo'-nah ah-bee-tah-syohn' mahs see-lehn-syoh'-
  sah?*

Do you have a room with a view of the ocean (court)?
¿Tiene una habitación con vista en el mar (patio)?
*Tyeh'-neh oo'-nah ah-bee-tah-syohn' kohn vees'-tah ehn
ehl mahr (pah'-tee-yoh)?*

What is the price of this róom?
¿Cuál es el precio de esta habitación?
Kwahl ehs ehl preh'-syoh deh eh'-stah ah-bee-tah-syohn'?

That's much too expensive.   **That's very good.**
Es demasiado cara.   Es muy bueno.
Ehs deh-mah-syah'-doh   *Ehs mwee bweh'-noh.*
  kah'-rah.

Does the price include breakfast?
¿Está incluído el desayuno en el precio?
*Eh-stah' een-kloo-ee'-doh ehl deh-sah-yoo'-noh ehn ehl
  preh'-syoh?*

Is there a restaurant at the hotel?
¿Hay un restaurante en el hotel?
Ah'-ee oon rehs-tow-rahn'-teh ehn ehl oh-tehl'?

Must we eat our meals in the hotel restaurant?
¿Tenemos que tomar las comidas en el restaurante del
hotel?
*Teh-neh'-mohs keh toh-mahr' lahs koh'mee'-dahs ehn
ehl rehs-tow-rahn'-teh dehl oh-tehl'?*

Where is the dining room?
¿Dónde está el comedor?
Dohn'-deh eh-stah' ehl koh-meh-dohr'?

We will stay here.
Nos quedaremos aquí.
Nohs keh-dah-reh'-mohs ah-kee'.

How long will you stay?
¿Cuánto tiempo se quedará usted?
Kwahn'-toh tyehm'-poh seh keh-dah-rah' oos-tehd'?

I will stay three weeks.
Me quedaré tres semanas.
Meh keh-dah-reh' trehs seh-mah'-nahs.

We will stay three weeks.
Nos quedaremos tres semanas.
Nohs keh-dah-reh'-mohs trehs seh-mah'-nahs.

Please fill out this card.
Sírvase llenar esta tarjeta.
Seer'-vah-seh lyeh-nahr' eh'-stah tahr-heh'-tah.

My key, please.
Mi llave, por favor.
Mee lyah'-veh, pohr fah-vohr'.

What number, sir?
¿Qué número, señor?
Keh noo'-meh-roh seh-nyohr'?

I have lost my key.
He perdido mi llave.
Eh pehr-dee'-doh mee lyah'-veh.

Where is the key to my room?
¿Dónde está la llave de mi habitación?
Dohn'-deh eh-stah' lah lyah'-veh deh mee ah-bee-tah-syohn'?

Where is the elevator?
¿Dónde está el ascensor?
Dohn'-deh eh-stah' ehl ahs-sehn-sohr'?

Take my suitcase to my room.
Suba mi maleta a mi habitación.
Soo'-bah mee mah-leh'-tah ah mee ah-bee-tah-syohn'.

Where is the bathroom?
¿Dónde está el cuarto de baño?
Dohn'-deh eh-stah' ehl kwahr'-toh deh bah'-nyoh?

Open the window, please.
Abra la ventana, por favor.
Ah'-brah lah vehn-tah'-nah, pohr fah-vohr'.

Close the window, please.
Cierre la ventana, por favor.
Syeh'-rreh lah vehn-tah'nah, pohr fah-vohr'.

Please call the chambermaid.
Llame a la camarera, por favor.
Lyah'-meh ah lah kah-mah-reh'-rah pohr fah-vohr'.

I want to have these shirts washed.
Quiero que se laven estas camisas.
Kyeh'-roh keh seh lah'-vehn eh'-stahs kah-mee'-sahs.

This is not my handkerchief.
Éste no es mi pañuelo.
Eh'-steh noh ehs mee pah-nyweh'-loh.

I want a towel and some soap.
Quiero una toalla y jabón.
Kyeh'-roh oo'-nah toh-ah'-lyah ee hah-bohn'.

I want a clean towel.
Quiero una toalla limpia.
Kyeh'-roh oo'-nah toh-ah'-lyah leem'-pyah.

Please wake me at seven o'clock.
Despiérteme a las siete, por favor.
Dehs-pyehr'-teh-meh ah lahs syeh'-teh, pohr fah-vohr'.

We are leaving tomorrow.
Salimos mañana.
Sah-lee'-mohs mah-nyah'-nah.

Take my luggage down.
Baje mi equipaje.
Bah'-hah mee eh-kee-pah'-heh.

Are there any letters for me?
¿Hay cartas para mí?
Ah'-ee kahr'-tahs pah'-rah mee?

I need some postage stamps.
Necesito unos sellos (unas estampillas).
Neh-seh-see'-toh oo'-nohs seh'-lyohs (oo'-nahs eh-stahm-pee'-lyahs).

Using the Telephone

Many visitors to foreign lands avoid using the telephone when they should not. Of course, gesturing and pointing are of no avail when you cannot see the person to whom you are speaking and have to depend entirely on what you hear and say. Still, it is possible to communicate if you make an effort. If there is difficulty, remember to ask the other person to speak slowly. It's your best assurance that the message will get through.

Where is there a telephone?
¿Dónde hay un teléfono?
Dohn'-deh ah'-ee oon teh-leh'-foh-noh?

I would like to telephone.
Quisiera telefonear.
Kee-syeh'-rah teh-leh-foh-neh-ahr'.

I would like to make a (long-distance) call to . . .
Quisiera hacer una llamada (de larga distancia) a . . .
Kee-syeh'-rah ah-sehr' oo'-nah yah-mah'-dah (deh lahr'-gah dees-tahn'-syah) ah . . .

What is the telephone number?
¿Cuál es el número telefónico?
Kwahl ehs ehl noo'-meh-roh teh-leh-foh'-nee-koh?

Where is the telephone book?
¿Dónde está la guía telefónica?
Dohn'-deh eh-stah' lah gee'-yah teh-leh-foh'-nee-kah?

My number is . . .	**Operator!**
Mi número es . . .	¡Telefonista!
Mee noo'-meh-roh ehs . . .	*Teh-leh-foh-nee'-stah!*

I want number . . .
Quiero el número . . .
Kyeh'-roh ehl noo'-meh-roh . . .

Can I dial this number?
¿Puedo marcar este número?
Pweh'-doh mahr-kahr' eh'-steh noo'-meh-roh?

How much is a telephone call to . . . ?
¿Cuánto cuesta una llamada telefónica a . . . ?
Kwahn'-toh kweh'-stah oo'-nah lyah-mah'-dah teh-leh-foh'-nee-kah ah . . . ?

I am ringing.	**He (she) is not in.**
Estoy sonando.	Él (Ella) no está.
Eh-stoy' soh-nahn'-doh.	*Ehl (eh'-lyah) noh eh-stah'.*

Please do not hang up.
No ponga el receptor, por favor.
Noh pohn'-gah ehl reh-sehp-tohr' pohr fah-vohr'.

Deposit coins.
Deposite moneda.
Deh-poh-see'-teh moh-neh'-dah.

They do not answer.
No contestan.
Noh kohn-teh'-stahn.

Please dial again.
Marque el número otra vez, por favor.
Mahr'-keh ehl noo'-meh-roh oh'-trah vehs, pohr fah-vohr'.

The line is busy.
La línea está ocupada.
Lah lee'-neh-ah eh-stah' oh-koo-pah'-dah.

Who is speaking?
¿Quién habla?
Kyehn ah'-blah?

May I speak to . . . ?
¿Puedo hablar con . . . ?
Pweh-doh ah-blahr' kohn...?

Please speak more slowly.
Hable más despacio, por favor.
Ah'-bleh mahs dehs-pah'-syoh, pohr fah-vohr'.

Getting Around by Taxi and Bus

The drivers of taxis and buses almost never speak English, which may be fortunate when you relish a few peaceful moments. However, you will have to tell them where you're going, or want to go, and for that we've provided some handy phrases.

Call a taxi, please.
Llame un taxi, por favor.
Lyah'-meh oon tak'-see, pohr fah-vohr'.

Put my luggage into the taxi.
Ponga mi equipaje en el taxi.
Pohn'-gah mee eh-kee-pah'-heh ehn ehl tak'-see.

Driver, are you free?
¿Chofer, está libre?
Choh'-fehr, eh-stah' lee'-breh?

Where do you wish to go?
¿Adónde desea ir?
Ah-dohn'-deh deh-seh'-ah eer?

Drive to the railroad station (airport).
Conduzca a la estación (al aeropuerto).
Kohn-doos'-kah ah lah eh-stah-syohn' (ahl ah-eh-roh-pwehr'-toh).

How much is the ride from here to the hotel?
¿Cuánto es el paseo de aquí al hotel?
Kwahn'-toh ehs ehl pah-seh'-oh deh ah-kee' ahl oh-tehl'?

Stop here!
¡Pare aquí!
Pah'-reh ah-kee'!

I want to get out here.
Quiero bajar aquí.
Kyeh'-roh bah-hahr' ah-kee'.

Wait until I come back.
Espere hasta que vuelva.
Eh-speh'-reh ah'-stah keh vwehl'-vah.

Wait for me here.
Espéreme aquí.
Eh-speh'-reh-meh ah-kee'.

Drive a little farther.
Siga un poco.
See'-gah oon poh'-koh.

Please drive carefully.
Maneje con cuidado, por favor.
Mah-neh'-heh kohn kwee-dah'-doh, pohr fah-vohr'.

Please drive slowly.
Maneje despacio, por favor.
Mah-neh'-heh dehs-pah'-syoh, pohr ʃah-vohr'.

Turn to the left (right) here.
Vuelva a la izquierda (derecha) aquí.
Vwehl'-vah ah lah ees-kyehr'-dah (deh-reh'-chah) ah-kee'.

Drive straight ahead.
Siga todo seguido.
See'-gah toh'-doh seh-gee'-doh.

How much is the fare?
¿Cuánto es la tarifa?
Kwahn'-toh ehs lah tah-ree'-fah?

Does the bus stop here?
Para el autobús aquí?
Pah'-rah ehl ow-toh-boos' ah-kee'?

Which bus goes downtown?
¿Cuál es el autobús que va al centro de la ciudad?
*Kwahl ehs ehl ow-toh-boos' keh vah ahl sehn'-troh deh lah
    syoo-dahd'?*

Bus number . . .
El autobús número . . .
Ehl ow-toh-boos' noo'-meh-roh . . .

Which bus goes to . . . ?
¿Cuál autobús va a . . . ?
Kwahl ow-toh-boos' vah ah . . . ?

Get on the bus here.
Suba en el autobús aquí.
*Soo'-bah ehn ehl ow-toh-
    boos' ah-kee'.*

Get off the bus here.
Baje del autobús aquí.
*Bah'heh dehl ow-toh-boos'
    ah-kee'.*

Please tell me when we arrive at . . . street.
Sírvase decirme cuando llegaremos a la calle . . .
*Seer'-vah-seh deh-seer'-meh kwahn'-doh lyah-gah-reh'-mohs
    ah lah kah'-lyeh . . .*

Does this bus go to the museum?
¿Va este autobús al museo?
Vah eh'-steh ow-toh-boos' ahl moo-seh'-oh?

Where must I transfer?
¿Dónde debo transbordar?
Dohn'-deh deh'-boh trahns-bohr-dahr'?

When does the last bus leave?
¿Cuándo sale el último autobús?
Kwahn'-doh sah'-leh ehl ool'-tee-moh ow-toh-boos'?

Eating and Drinking

Merely going abroad is thrill enough for some persons; for others the high points of a trip are likely to be the hours spent at the table. Getting to know and appreciate the national cuisine and learning how to order native dishes are extra thrills for many travelers. Here, along with the phrases that are necessary to order your meals, we have added a menu reader of the most typical dishes of the cuisine in the countries where Spanish is spoken.

I'm hungry.
Tengo hambre.
Tehn'-goh ahm'-breh.

Are you hungry?
¿Tiene usted hambre?
Tyeh'-neh oos-tehd' ahm'-breh?

I'm thirsty.
Tengo sed.
Tehn'-goh sehd.

Are you thirsty?
¿Tiene usted sed?
Tyeh'-neh oos-tehd' sehd?

I'm not hungry.
No tengo hambre.
Noh tehn'-goh ahm'-breh.

I'm not thirsty.
No tengo sed.
Noh tehn'-goh sehd.

Do you want to eat now?
¿Quiere usted comer ahora?
Kyeh'-reh oos-tehd' koh-mehr' ah-oh'-rah?

Let's eat now.
Comamos ahora.
Koh-mah'-mohs ah-oh'-rah.

Where is there a good restaurant?
¿Dónde hay un buen restaurante?
Dohn'-deh ah'-ee oon bwehn reh-stow-rahn'-teh?

The meals.
Las comidas.
Lahs koh-mee'-dahs.

breakfast
el desayuno
ehl deh-sah-yoo'-noh

lunch
el almuerzo
ehl ahl-mwehr'-soh

dinner
la comida
lah koh-mee'- dah

supper
la cena
lah seh'-nah

At what time is breakfast (lunch, dinner)?
¿A qué hora es el desayuno (el almuerzo, la comida)?
Ah keh oh'-rah ehs ehl deh-sah-yoo'-noh (ehl ahl-mwehr'-soh, lah koh-mee'-dah)?

I want breakfast (lunch, dinner) in my room.
Quiero el desayuno (el almuerzo, la comida) en mi habitación.
Kyeh'-roh ehl deh-sah-yoo'-noh (ehl ahl-mwehr'-soh, lah koh-mee'-dah) ehn mee ah-bee-tah-syohn'.

Breakfast is ready.
El desayuno está preparado.
Ehl deh-sah-yoo'-noh eh-stah' preh-pah-rah'-doh.

Dinner is being served.
La comida está servida.
Lah koh-mee'-dah eh-stah' sehr-vee'-dah.

A table for two, please.
Una mesa para dos, por favor.
Oo'-nah meh'-sah pah'-rah dohs, pohr fah-vohr'.

Where is the waitress?
¿Dónde está la moza?
Dohn'-deh eh-stah' lah moh'-sah?

Waiter (Waitress), the menu, please.
Mozo (Moza), la lista de los platos, por favor.
Moh'-soh (Moh'-sah), lah lees'-tah deh lohs plah'-tohs, pohr fah-vohr'.

Waiter, please bring an ashtray.
Mozo, traiga un cenicero, por favor.
Moh'-soh, trah'-ee-gah oon seh-nee-seh'-roh, pohr fah-vohr'.

What do you recommend?
¿Qué recomenda usted?
Keh reh-koh-mehn'-dah oos-tehd'?

Do you recommend . . . ?
¿Recomenda usted . . . ?
Reh-koh-mehn'-dah oos-tehd'. . . ?

Bring me some coffee now, please.
Tráigame café ahora, por favor.
Trah'-ee-gah-meh kah-feh' ah-or'-rah, pohr fah-vohr'.

More butter, please.
Más mantequilla, por favor.
Mahs mahn-teh-kee'-lyah, pohr fah-vohr'.

Bring some more sugar.
Traiga más azúcar.
Trah'-ee-gah mahs ah-soo'-kahr.

I would like . . .
Desearía . . .
Deh-seh-ah-ree'-yah. . . . .

eggs
huevos
weh'-vohs

fried eggs
huevos fritos
weh'-vohs free'-tohs

scrambled eggs
huevos revueltos
weh'-vohs reh-vwehl'-tohs

bacon
tocino
toh-see'-noh

two soft-boiled eggs
dos huevos pasados por agua
dohs weh'-vohs pah-sah'-dohs pohr ah'-gwah

a poached egg
un huevo escalfado
oon weh'-voh eh-skahl'-fah-doh

black coffee
café negro
keh-feh' neh'-groh

bread and butter
pan y mantequilla (manteca)
pahn ee mahn-teh-kee'-lyah (mahn-teh'-kah)

coffee without milk
café sin leche; café sólo
kah-feh' seen leh'cheh; kah-feh' soh'-loh

coffee with milk
cafe' con leche
kah-feh' kohn leh'-cheh

tea
el té
ehl teh

milk
la leche
lah leh'-cheh

cold meat
carne fría
kahr'-neh free'-yah

ham
jamón
hah-mohn'

rolls
panecillos
pahn-eh-see'-lyohs

Bring me a glass of water, please.
Tráigame un vaso de agua, por favor.
Trah'-ee-gah-meh oon vah'-soh deh ah'-gwah, pohr fah-vohr'.

This coffee is cold.
Este café está frío.
Eh'-steh kah-feh' eh-stah' free'-yoh.

Do you take milk and sugar?
Toma usted leche y azúcar?
Toh'-mah oos-tehd' leh'-cheh ee ah-soo'-kahr?

No sugar, thank you.
Ningún azúcar, gracias.
Neen-goon' ah-soo'-kahr, grah'-syahs.

We eat only fruit at breakfast.
Comemos sólo frutas al desayuno.
Koh-meh'-mohs soh'-loh froo'-tahs ahl deh-sah-yoo'-noh.

Condiments

the salt
la sal
lah sahl

the sugar
el azúcar
ehl ah-soo'-kahr

the vinegar
el vinagre
ehl vee-nah'-greh

the pepper
la pimienta
lah pee-myehn'-tah

the oil
el aceite
ehl ah-seh'-ee-teh

the mustard
la mostaza
lah mohs-tah'-sah

This butter is not fresh.
Esta mantequilla no está fresca.
Eh'-stah mahn-teh-kee'-lyah noh eh-stah' frehs'-kah.

This milk is warm.
Esta leche está caliente.
Eh'-stah leh'-cheh eh-stah' kah-lyehn'-teh.

This milk is sour.
Esta leche está agria.
Eh'-stah leh'-cheh eh-stah' ah'-gree-yah.

I would like a glass of cold milk.
Quisiera un vaso de leche fría.
Kee-syeh'-rah oon vah'-soh deh leh'-cheh free'-yah.

Another cup of coffee?
¿Otra taza de café?
Oh'-trah tah'-sah deh kah-feh'?

Another cup of tea?
¿Otra taza de té?
Oh-trah tah'-sah deh teh?

Do you want some more tea?
¿Quiere usted más té?
Kyeh'-reh oos-tehd' mahs teh?

Foods and Beverages

the fish
el pescado
ehl pehs-kah'-doh

fruit
la fruta, las frutas
lah froo'-tah, lahs froot'-tahs

the meat
la carne
lah kahr'-neh

the soup
la sopa
lah soh'-pah

vegetables
los legumbres
lohs leh-goom'-brehs

the water
el agua
ehl ah'-gwah

the wine
el vino
ehl vee'-noh

the beer
la cerveza
lah sehr-veh'-sah

Nothing more, thank you.
Nada más, gracias.
Nah'-dah mahs, grah'-syahs.

At what time are the meals in this hotel?
¿A qué hora se sirven las comidas en este hotel?
Ah keh oh'-rah seh seer'-vehn lahs koh-mee'-dahs ehn eh'-steh oh-tehl'?

We dine at seven o'clock.
Comemos a las siete.
Koh-meh'-mohs ah lahs syeh'-teh.

Here they dine at eight o'clock.
Aquí se come a las ocho.
Ah-kee' seh koh'-meh ah lahs oh'-choh.

Please reserve a table for us.
Reserve una mesa para nosotros, por favor.
Reh-sehr'-veh oo'-nah meh'-sah pah'-rah noh-soh'-trohs, pohr fah-vohr'.

the cheese	**the bread**
el queso	el pan
ehl keh'-soh	*ehl pahn*
the butter	**the milk**
la mantequilla	la leche
lah mahn-teh-kee'-lyah	*lah leh'-cheh*
the jam	**the honey**
la conserva	la miel
lah kohn-sehr'-vah	*lah myehl*
the salad	
la ensalada	
lah ehn-sah-lah'-dah	

Do you want soup?
¿Desea usted sopa?
Deh-seh'-ah oos-tehd' soh'-pah?

Bring me a fork (a knife, a spoon).
Tráigame un tenedor (un cuchillo, una cuchara).
*Trah'-ee-gah-meh oon teh-neh-dohr' (oon koo-chee'-lyoh,
oo'-nah koo-chah'-rah).*

This fork is dirty.
Este tenedor está sucio.
*Eh'-steh teh-neh-dohr' eh-
stah' soo'-syoh.*

This spoon isn't clean.
Esta cuchara no está limpia.
*Eh'-stah koo-chah'-rah noh
eh-stah' leem'-pyah.*

Please bring me a napkin.
Tráigame una servilleta, por favor.
*Trah'-ee-gah-meh oo'-nah sehr-vee-lyeh'-tah, pohr
fah-vohr'.*

The Setting

a spoon
una cuchara
oo'-nah koo-chah'-rah

a small spoon
una cucharita
oo'-nah koo-chah'-ee-tah

a knife
un cuchillo
oon koo-chee'-lyoh

a fork
un tenedor
oon teh-neh-dohr'

a small knife
un cuchillo pequeño
*oon koo-chee'-lyoh peh-
keh'-nyoh*

a small fork
un tenedor pequeño
*oon teh-neh-dohr' peh-keh'-
nyoh*

a plate
un plato
oon plah'-toh

a tray
una bandeja
oo'-nah bahn-deh'-hah

a napkin
una servilleta
oo'-nah sehr-vee-lyeh'-tah

I would like a glass of wine.
Quisiera un vaso de vino.
Kee-syeh'-rah oon vah'-soh deh vee'-noh.

A glass of red (white) wine.
Un vaso de vino tinto (blanco).
Oon vah'-soh deh vee'-noh teen'-toh (blahn'-koh).

A bottle of wine.
Una botella de vino.
Oo'-nah boh-teh'-lyah deh vee'-noh.

This wine is too warm.
Este vino está demasiado caliente.
Eh'-steh vee'-noh eh-stah' deh-mah-syah'-doh kah-lyehn'-teh.

A half-bottle.
Una media botella.
Oo'-nah meh'-dee-yah boh-tehl'-yah.

Please bring some ice.
Traiga un poco de hielo, por favor.
Trah'-ee-gah oon poh'-koh deh yeh'-loh, pohr fah-vohr'.

I didn't order this.
No pedí éste.
Noh peh-dee' eh'-steh.

A glass of beer.
Un vaso de cerveza.
Oon vah'-soh deh sehr-veh'-sah.

A bottle of beer.
Una botella de cerveza.
Oo'-nah boh-teh'-lyah deh sehr-veh'-sah.

To your health!
¡Salud!
Sah-lood'!

Enjoy your meal!
¡Buen apetito!
Bwehn ah-peh-tee'-toh!

This tablecloth is not clean.
Este mantel no está limpio.
Eh-steh mahn-tehl' noh eh-stah' leem'-pyoh.

Do you eat fish?
¿Come usted pescado?
Koh'-meh oos-tehd' pehs-kah'-doh?

He doesn't eat meat.
Él no come carne.
Ehl noh koh'-meh kahr'-neh.

I don't eat dessert.
Yo no como postres.
Yoh noh koh'-moh pohs'-trehs.

He would like some ice cream.
Él quiere helado.
Ehl kyeh'-reh eh-lah'-doh.

Waiter, the check, please.
Mozo, la cuenta, por favor.
Moh'-soh, lah kwehn'-tah, pohr fah-vohr'

How much do I owe you?
¿Cuánto le debo?
Kwahn'-toh leh deh'-boh?

Is the tip included?
¿Está incluído el servicio?
Eh-stah' een-kloo-ee'-doh ehl sehr-vee'-syoh?

Where do I pay?
¿Dónde pago?
Dohn'-deh pah'-goh?

At the cashier's booth.
En la caja.
Ehn lah kah'-hah.

I have already paid.
Ya he pagado.
Yah eh pah-gah'-doh.

Here is a tip.
He aquí una propina.
Eh ah-kee' oo'-nah proh-pee'-nah.

I left the tip on the table.
Dejé la propina en la mesa.
Deh-heh' lah proh-pee'-nah ehn lah meh'-sah.

There is a mistake in the bill.
Hay un error en la cuenta.
Ah'-ee oon eh-rrohr' ehn lah kwehn'-tah.

Menu
Reader

Sopas y Aperitivos Soups and Appetizers

Caldo (*kahl'-doh*) Chicken broth.

Entremeses (*ehn-treh-meh'-sehs*) Hor d'oeuvres.

Gazpacho (*gahs-pah'-choh*) Chilled seasoned vegetable soup. A Spanish specialty.

Sopa clara (*soh'-pah klah'-rah*) Consommé.

Sopa de ajo (*soh'-pah deh ah'-hoh*) Garlic soup.

Sopa de albóndigas (*soh'-pah deh ahl-bohn'-dee-gahs*) Tomato base soup with meatballs.

Sopa de legumbres (*soh'-pah deh leh-goom'-brehs*) Vegetable soup.

Sopa española (*soh'-pah eh-spah-nyoh'-lah*) Spiced soup with rice, tomatoes, and peppers.

Pescado y Mariscos Fish and Shellfish

Almejas (*ahl-meh'-hahs*) Clams.
Gambas (*gahm'-bahs*) Large shrimp.
Langosta (*lahn-goh'-stah*) A variety of lobster.
Paella (*pah-eh'-lyah*) Assorted seafood and meats and yellow rice. A Spanish specialty.
Salmón ahumado (*sahl-mohn' ah-oo-mah'-doh*) Smoked salmon.

Carne y Aves Meat and Poultry

Arroz con pollo (*ah-rrohs' kohn poh'-lyoh*) Chicken with rice. A Spanish specialty.
Biftec (*beef'-tehk*) Steak.
   poco hecho (*poh'-koh eh'-choh*) Rare.
   muy hecho (*mwee eh'-choh*) Well done.
Caldo gallego (*kahl'-doh gah-lyeh'-goh*) Thick stew with meat and vegetables.
Chuletas de cerdo (*choo-leh'-tahs deh sehr'-doh*) Pork cutlets.
Chuletas de cordero (*choo-leh'-tahs deh kohr-deh'-roh*) Lamb cutlets.
Chuletas de ternera (*choo-leh'-tahs deh tehr-neh'-rah*) Veal cutlets.
Costillas de cordero (*koh-stee'-lyahs deh kohr-deh'-roh*) Lamb chops.
Empanadas (*ehm-pah-nah'-dahs*) Meat pies.
Enchiladas (*ehn-chee-lah'-dahs*) Mexican corn cake with a meat, cheese, and chile stuffing.
Guisado español (*gee-sah'-doh eh-spah-nyohl'*) Beef stew with onions in olive oil.
Jamón aguadilla (*hah-mohn' ah-gwah-dee'-lyah*) Roast fresh ham.
Rosbif (*rohs-beef'*) Roast beef.
Salchichas (*Sahl-chee'-chahs*) Veal and pork sausage.

Tamale (*tah-mah'-leh*) Seasoned ground meat rolled in cornmeal dough and steamed or fried.

Tortilla (*tohr-tee'-lyah*) In Mexico, a thin, unleavened corn cake; in Spain, an omelet.

Legumbres y Ensaladas Vegetables and Salads

Cebolla (*seh-boh'-lyah*) Onion.

Ensalada de pepino (*ehn-sah-lah'-dah deh peh-pee'-noh*) Cucumber salad.

Ensalada variada (*ehn-sah-lah'-dah vah-ree-ah'-dah*) Mixed green salad.

Favas (*fah'-vahs*) Lima beans.

Guisantes (*gee-sahn'-tehs*) Peas.

Habichuelas (*ah-bee-chweh'-lahs*) Beans.

Judías verdes (*hoo-dee'-ahs vehr'-dehs*) String beans.

Lechuga (*leh-choo'-gah*) Lettuce.

Papas (*pah'-pahs*) Potatoes.

Patatas (*pah-tah'-tahs*) Potatoes.

Tomate (*toh-mah'-teh*) Tomato.

Postres y Frutas Desserts and Fruits

Cerezas (*seh-reh'-sahs*) Cherries.

Compota (*kohm-poh'-tah*) Stewed fruit.

Durasno (*doo-rahs'-noh*) Peach.

Flan (*flahn*) Caramel custard. A Spanish specialty.

Frambuesas (*frahm-bweh'-sahs*) Raspberries.
  con nata (*kohn nah'-tah*) With cream.

Fresas (*freh'-sahs*) Strawberries.

Helados (*eh-lah'-dohs*) Ice cream.

Melocotón (*meh-loh-koh-tohn'*) Peach.

Piña (*pee'-nyah*) Pineapple.

Queso (*keh'-soh*) Cheese.

Tarta (*tahr'-tah*) Tart, pie.

Torta, (*tohr'-tah*) Cake.

Bebidas Beverages

Agua (*ah'-gwah*) Water.
Agua gaseosa (*ah'-gwah gah-seh-oh-sah*) Soda water.
Agua natural (*ah'-gwah nah-too-rahl'*) Plain water.
Café (*kah-fah'*) Coffee.
   con leche (*kohn leh'-cheh*) With milk.
   negro (*neh'-groh*) Black coffee.
   sin leche (*seen leh'-cheh*) Without milk.
Cerveza (*sehr-veh'-sah*) Beer.
Jérez (*heh'-rehs*) Sherry.
Jugo (*hoo'-goh*) Juice.
Jugo de naranja (*hoo'-goh deh nah-rahn'-hah*) Orange juice.
Leche (*leh'-cheh*) Milk.
Pulque (*pool'-keh*) Strong, fermented drink made from the Mexican maguey plant.
Sangría (*sahn-gree'-ah*) Mild fruit punch made with vermouth. A Spanish specialty.
Vino (*vee'-noh*) Wine.
Vino blanco (*vee'-noh blahn'-koh*) White wine.
Vino tinto (*vee'-noh teen'-toh*) Red wine.

Shopping

Shopping abroad is always an adventure and frequently a delight. It's not only the varied merchandise that you may buy to take home as gifts, but the sheer pleasure of making yourself understood. It's important to know, and to be able to explain, exactly what it is that you want, since, obviously, you won't be able to trot downtown a week later to make an exchange. You'll discover, too, that sizes and weights are different; so we have included conversion tables here. Here are the typical questions that you or the salesman might ask or the statement you may make during your shopping trips.

I would like to go shopping.
Quisiera ir de compras.
Kee-syeh'-rah eer deh kohm'-prahs.

At what time do the stores open?
¿A qué hora se abren las tiendas?
Ah keh oh'-rah seh ah'-brehn lahs tyehn'-dahs?

At what time do the stores close?
¿A qué hora se cierran las tiendas?
(Ah keh oh'-rah seh syeh'-rrahn lahs tyehn'-dahs?

Where is there . . . ?
¿Dónde hay . . . ?
Dohn'-deh ah'-ee . . . ?

an antique shop.
una tienda de antigüedades.
oo'-nah tyehn'-dah deh ahn-tee-gweh-dah'-dehs.

a book store.
una librería.
oo'-nah lee-breh-ree'-yah.

a candy store.
una confitería.
oo'-nah kohn-fee-teh-ree'-yah.

a department store.
un almacén.
oon ahl-mah-sehn'.

a dressmaker.
una modista.
oo'-nah moh-dees'-tah.

a druggist.
un farmacista.
oon fahr-mah-sees'-tah.

a drugstore.
una farmacia.
oo'-nah fahr-mah'-syah.

a florist.
un florero.
oon floh-reh'-roh.

a greengrocer.
un verdulero.
oon vehr-doo-leh'-roh.

a grocery.
una tienda de comestibles.
oo'-nah tyehn'-dah deh koh-mehs-tee'-blehs.

a hat shop.
una sombrerería.
oo'-nah sohm-breh-reh-ree'-yah.

a jewelry store.
una joyería.
oo'-nah hoh-yeh-ree'-yah.

May I help you?
¿En qué puedo servirle?
Ehn keh pweh'-doh sehr-veer'-leh?

Will you help me, please?
¿Me servirá usted, por favor?
Meh sehr-veer-ah' oos-tehd', pohr fah-vohr'?

Are you being served?   **What do you wish?**
¿Le sirven a usted?   ¿Qué desea usted?
Leh seer'-vehn ah oost-tehd'?   Ken deh-seh'-ah oos-tehd'?

---

a perfumery.
una perfumería.
oo'-nah pehr-foo-meh-ree'-yah.

a photography shop.
una fotografería.
oo'-nah foh-toh-grah-feh-ree'-yah.

a shoe store.   **a tailor.**
una zapatería.   un sastre.
oo'-nah sah-pah-teh-ree'-yah.   oon sahs'-treh.

a tobacconist.
una tabaquería.
oo'-nah tah-bah-keh-ree'-yah.

a toy store.
una tienda de juguetes.
oo'-nah tyehn'-dah deh hoo-geh'-tehs.

a watchmaker.
un relojero.
oon reh-loh-heh'-roh.

I would like . . .
Desearía . . .
Deh-seh-ah-ree'-yah . . .

I would like . . .
Quisiera . . .
Kee-syeh'-rah . . .

a brassiere.
un sostén
oon sohs-tehn'

gloves.
guantes
gwahn'-tehs

a handkerchief.
un pañuelo
oon pah-nyweh'-loh

a hat.
un sombrero
oon sohm-breh'-roh

panties.
calzones
kahl-soh'-nehs

a shirt.
una camisa
oo'-nah kah-mee'-sah

shoes.
zapatos
sah-pah'-tohs

shorts.
calzoncillos
kahl-sohn-see'-lyohs

a skirt.
una falda
oo'-nah fahl'-dah

a slip.
una combinación
oo'-nah kohm-bee-nah-syohn'

socks.
calcetines
kahl-seh-tee'-nehs

stockings.
medias
meh'-dee-yahs

a suit.
un traje
oon trah'-heh

a sweater.
un suéter
oon sweh'-tehr

a tie.
una corbata
oo'-nah kohr-bah'-tah

an undershirt
una camisola, camiseta
oo'-nah kah-mee-soh'-lah kah-mee-seh'-tah

underwear.
ropa interior
roh'-pah een-teh-ree-ohr'

I would like to buy . . .
Desearía comprar . . .
Deh-seh-ah-ree'-yah kohm-prahr' . . .

---

a battery.
una batería
oo'-nah bah-teh-ree'-yah

a camera.
una cámara
oo'-nah kah'-mah-rah

film.
película
peh-lee'-koo-lah

flashbulbs.
bombillas de cámara
bohm-bee'-lyahs deh kah'-mah-rah

a pen.
una pluma
oo'-nah ploo'-mah

a pencil.
un lápiz
oon lah'-pees

postcards.
tarjetas postales
tahr-heh'-tahs poh-stah'-lehs

stamps.
estampillas; sellos
eh-stahm-pee'-lyahs; seh'-lyohs

lotion.
loción
loh-syohn'

powder.
polvos
pohl'-vohs

razor blades.
hojitas de afeitar
oh-hee'-tahs deh ah-feh-ee-tahr'

shampoo.
champú
chahm-poo'

shaving cream.
crema de afeitar
kreh'-mah deh ah-feh-ee-tahr'

soap.
jabón
hah-bohn'

toothbrush.
cepillo de dientes
seh-pee'-lyoh deh dyehn'-tehs

toothpaste.
pasta dentífrica
pah'-stah dehn-tee'-free-kah

I would like to buy . . .
Quisiera comprar . . .
Kee-syeh'-rah kohm-prahr' . . .

cigar. puro *poo'-roh*	**cigarettes.** cigarrillos *see-gah-rree'-lyohs*
flint. pedernal *peh-dehr-nahl'*	**fluid.** líquido *lee'-kee-doh*
lighter. encendedor *ehn-sehn-deh-dohr'*	**matches.** fósforos *fohs'-foh-rohs*

Do you sell . . . ?
¿Vende usted . . . ?
Vehn'-deh oos-tehd' . . . ?

Do you have. . . ?
¿Tiene usted . . . ?
Tyeh'-neh oos-tehd' . . . ?

Please show me some . . .
Sírvase mostrarme unos (unas) . . .
Seer'-vah-seh moh-strahr'-meh oo'-nohs (oo'-nahs) . . .

I would like to see some dresses.
Quisiera ver unos vestidos.
Kee-syeh'-rah vehr oo'-nohs vehs-tee'-dohs.

What size, please?
¿Qué medida, por favor?
Keh meh-dee'-dah, pohr fah-vohr'?

Try on these . . .
Pruebe éstos (éstas) . . .
Prweh'-beh eh'-stohs (eh'-stahs) . . .

How much does it cost?
¿Cuánto cuesta?
Kwahn'-toh kweh'-stah?

How much do they cost?
¿Cuánto cuestan?
Kwahn'-toh kweh'-stahn?

That is too expensive.
Es demasiado caro.
Ehs deh-ma-syah'-doh kah'-roh.

That is cheap.
Es barato.
Ehs bah-rah'-toh.

I like this one.
Me gusta éste (ésta).
Meh goo'-stah eh'steh (eh'-stah.)

I will take this one.
Me quedo con éste (ésta).
Meh keh'-doh kohn eh'-steh eh'-stah.

I don't like this color.
No me gusta este color.
Noh meh goo'-stah eh'-steh koh-lohr'.

I prefer it in . . .
Lo prefiero en . . .
Loh preh-fyeh'-roh ehn . . .

black	**blue**	**brown**
negro	azul	pardo
neh'-groh	*ah-sool'*	*pahr'-doh*
gray	**green**	**red**
gris	verde	rojo
grees	*vehr'-deh*	*roh'-hoh*
white	**yellow**	
blanco	amarillo	
blahn'-koh	*ah-mah-ree'-lyoh*	
dark	**light**	
oscuro	claro	
oh-skoo'-roh	*klah'-roh*	

Sale
Venta
Vehn'-tah

For Sale
De Venta
Deh vehn'-tah

Clearance Sale
Saldo
Sahl'-doh

This dress is too short.
Este vestido está demasiado corto.
Eh'-steh vehs-tee'-doh eh-stah' deh-mah-syah'-doh kohr'-toh.

This skirt is too long.
Esta falda está demasiado larga.
Eh'-stah fahl'-dah eh-stah' deh-mah-syah'-doh lahr'-gah.

I would like to see a white shirt.
Quisiera ver una camisa blanca.
Kee-syeh'-rah vehr oo'-nah kah-mee'-sah blahn'-kah.

He would like to see some white shirts.
Él quisiera ver unas camisas blancas.
Ehl kee-syeh'-rah vehr oo'-nahs kah-mee'-sahs blahn'-kahs.

The sleeves are too wide.
Las mangas están demasiado anchas.
Lahs mahn'-gahs eh-stahn' deh-mah-syah'-doh ahn'-chahs

The sleeves are too narrow.
Las mangas están demasiado estrechas.
Lahs mahn'-gahs eh-stahn' deh-mah-syah'-doh eh-streh'-chahs.

I would like to see some shoes.
Quisiera ver unos zapatos.
Kee-syeh'-rah vehr oo'-nohs sah-pah'-tohs.

A pair of black (brown) shoes.
Un par de zapatos negros (pardos).
Oon pahr deh sah-pah'-tohs neh'-grohs (pahr'-dohs).

Try this pair on.
Pruebe este par.
Prweh'-beh eh'-steh pahr.

They are too narrow.
Están demasiado estrechos.
*Eh-stahn' deh-mah-syah'-
doh eh-streh'-chohs.*

They are too tight (loose).
Son demasiado apretados (flojos).
Sohn deh-mah-syah'-doh ah-preh-tah'-dohs (floh'-hohs).

They are not big enough.
No son bastante grandes.
Noh sohn bah-stahn'-teh grahn'-dehs.

They are too long (short).
Son demasiado largos (cortos).
Sohn deh-mah-syah'-doh lahr'-gohs (kohr'-tohs).

Do you sell cigarettes?
¿Vende usted cigarrillos?
*Vehn'-deh oos-tehd' see-
gah-rree'-lyohs?*

Do you have matches?
¿Tiene usted fósforos?
*Tyeh'-neh oos-tehd' fohs'-
foh-rohs?*

I want to buy needles, pins, and some thread.
Quiero comprar agujas, alfileres y algo de hilo.
*Kyeh'-roh kohm-prahr' ah-goo'-hahs ahl-fee-leh'-rehs ee
ahl'-goh deh ee'-loh.*

How many do you want?
¿Cuántos quiere usted?
*Kwahn'-tohs kyeh'-reh oos-
tehd'?*

Anything else?
¿Otra cosa? ¿Algo más?
*Oh'-trah koh'-sah? Ahl'-
goh mahs?*

No thank you. That's all.
No, gracias. Eso es todo.
Noh, grah'-syahs. Eh'-soh ehs toh'-doh.

I'll take it (them) with me.
Me lo (los) llevo.
Meh loh (lohs) lyeh'-voh.

Will you wrap it, please?
Lo envolverá, por favor?
Loh ehn-vohl-veh-rah', pohr fah-vohr'.

Send it to the hotel.
Mándelo(Envíelo) al hotel.
Mahn'-deh-loh (ehn-vee'-eh-loh) ahl oh-tehl'.

Pack it (them) for shipment to . . .
Empáquelo (Empáquelos) para enviar a . . .
Ehm-pah'-keh-loh (ehm-pah'-keh-lohs) pah'-rah ehn-vee-yahr' ah . . .

Here is the bill.
He aquí la cuenta.
Eh ah-kee' lah kwehn'-tah.

I will pay cash.
Pagaré al contado.
Pah-gah-reh' ahl kohn-tah'-doh.

Is there a discount?
¿Hay un descuento?
Ah'-ee oon dehs-kwehn'-toh?

CLOTHING SIZE CONVERSIONS: *Women*

Dresses, Suits and Coats

American:		8	10	12	14	16	18
British:		30	32	34	36	38	40
Continental:		36	38	40	42	44	46

Blouses and Sweaters

American:	32	34	36	38	40	42	44
British:	34	36	38	40	42	44	46
Continental:	40	42	44	46	48	50	52

Stockings

American and British:		8	8½	9	9½	10	10½	11
Continental:		35	36	37	38	39	40	41

Shoes

American:	5	5½	6	6½	7	7½	8	8½	9
British:	3½	4	4½	5	5½	6	6½	7	7½
Continental:	35	35	36	37	38	38	38½	39	40

Gloves

American, British and Continental sizes are the same

CLOTHING SIZE CONVERSIONS: *Men*

Suits, Sweaters and Overcoats

American and British:	34	36	38	40	42	44	46	48
Continental:	44	46	48	50	52	54	56	58

Shirts

American and British:	14	14½	15	15½	16	16½	17	17½
Continental:		36	37	38	39	40	41	42	43

Socks

American and British:	9½	10	10½	11	11½	12	12½
Continental:	39	40	41	42	43	44	45

Shoes

American:	7	7½	8	8½	9	9½	10	10½	11	11½
British:	6½	7	7½	8	8½	9	9½	10	10½	11
Continental:	39	40	41	42	43	43	44	44	45	45

Getting Around by Automobile

Since few attendants who work at garages and stations speak English, some ability in Spanish will be very useful. You will need gasoline, of course, and probably some regular servicing. And should there be some problem with the car, a lot of time and energy will be saved if you can explain your needs.

I would like to hire a car.
Quisiera alquilar un coche.
Kee-syeh'-rah ahl-kee-lahr' oon koh'-cheh.

How much does a car cost per day?
¿Cuánto cuesta un coche por día?
Kwahn'-toh kweh'-stah oon koh'-cheh pohr dee'-yah?

How much per kilometer?
¿Cuánto por kilómetro?
Kwahn'-toh pohr kee-loh'-meh-troh?

Is gasoline expensive in this country?
¿Es cara la gasolina en este país?
Ehs keh'-rah lah gah-soh-lee'-nah ehn eh'-steh pah-ees'?

Is there a deposit?
¿Hay un depósito?
Ah'-ee oon deh-poh'-see'-toh?

I would like a car with seatbelts and an outside mirror, please.
Quisiera un coche con cinturones de asiento y un espejo exterior, por favor.
Kee-syeh'-rah oon koh'-cheh kohn seen-too-roh'-nehs deh ah-syehn'-toh ee oon ehs-peh'-hoh ehs-teh-ree-yohr', pohr fah-vohr'.

I will (will not) take the car out of the country.
Tomaré (no tomaré) el coche fuera del país.
Toh-mah-reh' (*noh toh-mah-reh'*) *ehl koh'-cheh fweh'-rah dehl pah-ees'.*

I want to leave it in . . .
Quiero dejarlo en . . .
Kyeh'-roh deh-hahr'-loh ehn . . .

How much is the insurance per day?
¿Cuánto es el seguro al día?
Kwahn'-toh ehs ehl seh-goo'-roh ahl dee'-yah?

Here is the registration and the key.
Aquí está el registro y la llave.
Ah-kee' eh-stah' ehl reh-hees'-troh ee lah lyah'-veh.

Where is there a gas station?
¿Dónde hay un puesto de gasolina?
Dohn'-deh ah'-ee oon pweh'-stoh deh gah-soh-lee'-nah?

Fill it up.
Llénelo.
Lyeh'-neh-loh.

Premium.
Superior.
Soo-peh-ree-yohr'.

Regular.
Ordinario.
Ohr-dee-nah'-ree-yoh.

I want twenty liters of gasoline.
Quiero veinte litros de gasolina.
Kyeh'-roh veh'-een-teh lee'-trohs deh gah-soh-lee'-nah.

I also need some oil.
Necesito aceite también.
Neh-seh-see'-toh ah-seh'-ee-teh tahm-byehn'.

Please put in some water.
Ponga un poco de agua, por favor.
Pohn'-gah oon poh'-koh deh ah'-gwah, pohr fah-vohr'.

Please inspect the tires.
Revise las llantas, por favor.
Reh-vee'-seh lahs lyahn'-tahs, pohr fah-vohr'.

Wash the car, please.
Lave el coche, por favor.
Lah'-veh ehl koh'-cheh, pohr fah-vohr'.

Put in some air.
Ponga aire.
Pohn'-gah ah'-ee-reh.

Is there a mechanic here?
¿Hay un mecánico aquí?
Ah'-ee oon meh-kah'-nee-koh ah-kee'?

Can you fix a flat tire?
¿Puede reparar un pinchazo (una llanta desinflada)?
Pweh'-deh reh-pah-rahr' oon peen-chah'-soh (oo'-nah lyahn'-tah deh-seen-flah'-dah)?

How long will it take?
¿Cuanto tiempo tardará?
Kwahn'-toh tyehm'-poh tahr-dah-rah'?

Have you a road map?
¿Tiene usted un mapa de las carreteras?
Tyeh'-neh oos-tehd' oon mah'-pah deh lahs kah-rreh-teh'-rahs?

Where does this road go to?
¿Adónde va esta carretera?
Ah-dohn'-deh vah eh'-stah kah-rreh-teh'-rah?

Is this the road to . . . ?
¿Es ésta la carretera a . . . ?
Ehs eh'-stah lah kah-rreh-teh'-rah ah . . . ?

A narrow road.
Una carretera estrecha.
Oo'-nah kah-rreh-teh'-rah eh-streh'-chah.

A wide road.
Una carretera ancha.
Oo'-nah kah-rreh-teh'-rah ahn'-chah.

A narrow bridge.
Un puente estrecho.
Oon pwehn'-teh eh-streh'-choh.

A bad road.
Una mala carretera.
Oo'-nah mah'-lah kah-rreh-teh'-rah.

Is the road good?
¿Es buena la carretera?
Ehs bweh'-nah lah kah-rreh-teh'-rah?

This road is slippery when it's wet.
Esta carretera está resbalosa cuando está mojada.
Eh'-stah kah-rreh-teh'-rah eh-stah' reh-bah-loh'-sah kwahn'-doh eh-stah' moh-hah'-dah.

Where is the nearest garage?
¿Dónde está el garage más proximo?
Dohn'-deh eh-stah' ehl gah-rah'-heh mahs prohk'-see-moh?

Is there a speed limit here?
¿Hay un límite de velocidad aquí?
Ah'-ee oon lee'-mee-teh deh veh-loh-see-dahd' ah-kee'?

You were driving too fast.
Usted manejaba muy de prisa.
Oos-tehd' mah-neh-hah'-bah mwee deh pree'-sah.

You must pay the fine.
Debe pagar la multa.
Deh'-beh pah-gahr' lah mool'-tah.

May I leave the car here?
¿Puedo dejar el coche aquí?
*Pweh'-doh deh-hahr' ehl
    koh'-cheh ah-kee'?*

May I park here?
¿Puedo estacionar aquí?
*Pweh'-doh eh-stah-syoh-
    nahr' ah-kee'?*

I have a driver's license.
Tengo una licencia de manejar.
Tehn'-goh oo'-nah lee-sehn'-syah deh mah-neh-hahr'.

Please check . . .
Revise . . . por favor.
Reh-vee'-seh . . . pohr fah-vohr'.

This car isn't running well.
Este coche no marcha bien.
Eh'-steh koh'-cheh noh mahr'-chah byehn.

Can you fix it?
¿Puede usted repararlo?
*Pweh'-deh oos-tehd' reh-
    pah-rahr'-loh?*

How long will it take?
¿Cuánto tiempo tardará?
*Kwahn'-toh tyehm'-poh
    tahr-dah-rah'?*

Your car is ready.
Su coche está listo.
*Soo koh'-cheh eh-stah'
    lee'-stoh.*

Drive carefully!
¡Maneje con cuidado!
*Mah-neh'-heh kohn kwee-
    dah'-doh!*

Please wipe the windshield.
Limpie el parabrisas, por favor.
Leem'-pyeh ehl pah-rah-bree'-sahs, pohr fah-vohr.

I don't know what the matter is.
No sé lo que hay.
Noh seh loh keh ah'-ee.

I think it's . . .	Is it . . .?
Creo que es . . .	¿Es . . . ?
Kreh'-oh keh ehs . . .	*Ehs . . . ?*

the accelerator.
el acelerador
ehl ah-seh-leh-rah-dohr'

the air filter.
el filtro de aire
ehl feel'-troh deh ah'-ee-reh

the battery.
la batería
lah bah-teh-ree'-yah

the brakes.
los frenos
lohs freh'-nohs

the carburetor.
el carburador
ehl kahr-boo-rah-dohr'

the clutch.
el embrague
ehl ehm-brah'-geh

the lights.
las luces
lahs loo'-sehs

the motor.
el motor
ehl moh-tohr'

the spark plugs.
las bujías
lahs boo-hee'-ahs

the tires.
las llantas
lahs lyahn'-tahs

the wheel.
la rueda
lah rweh'-dah

the wheels.
las ruedas
lahs rweh'-dahs

the front wheel.
la rueda delantera
lah rweh'-dah deh-lahn-teh'-rah

the back wheel.
la rueda posterior
lah rweh'-dah pohs-teh-ree-ohr'

Priority road ahead

Stop

Dangerous curve

Right curve

Double curve

Intersection

Intersection with secondary road

Railroad crossing
with gates

Railroad crossing
without gates

Road work

Pedestrian
crossing

Children

Road narrows

Uneven road

Slippery road

Traffic circle
ahead

Danger

Closed to
all vehicles

No entry

No left turn

No U turn

Overtaking
prohibited

Speed limit

Customs

No parking

Direction to
be followed

Traffic circle

No parking

Getting Around by Train

The railroad is the most frequently used means of transportation by visitors abroad. Schedules and timetables are usually readily understandable — if they are visible — but otherwise, in arranging your travel by train, you will need to use some of these phrases.

The railroad station.
La estación de ferrocarriles.
Lah eh-stah-syohn' deh feh-rroh-kah-rree'-lehs.

The train.
El tren.
Ehl trehn.

Drive to the railroad station.
Vaya a la estación.
Vah'-yah ah lah eh-stah-syohn'.

I need a porter.
Necesito un mozo (portero).
Neh-seh-see'-toh oon moh'-soh (pohr-teh'-roh).

Porter, here is my luggage.
Portero, aquí está mi equipaje.
Pohr-teh-roh, ah-kee' eh-stah' mee eh-kee-pah'-heh.

These are my bags.
Éstas son mis maletas.
Eh'-stahs sohn mees mah-leh'-tahs.

Here are the baggage checks.
He aquí los talones (las contraseñas).
Eh ah-kee' lohs tah-loh'-nehs (lahs kohn-trah-seh'-nyahs).

Where is the ticket window?
¿Dónde está el despacho de billetes?
Dohn'-deh eh-stah' ehl deh-spah'-choh deh bee-lyeh'-tehs?

Have you a timetable?
¿Tiene usted un horario?
Tyeh'-neh oos-tehd' oon oh-rah'-ree-oh?

When does the train leave?
¿Cuándo sale el tren?
Kwahn'-doh sah'-leh ehl trehn?

From which platform?
¿De qué plataforma?
Deh keh plah-tah-fohr'-mah?

I want a ticket to . . .
Quiero un billete para . . .
Kyeh'-roh oon bee-lyeh'-teh pah'-rah . . .

I want to check this baggage.
Quiero facturar este equipaje.
Kyeh'-roh fahk-too-rahr' eh'-steh eh-kee-pah'-heh.

I must pick up a ticket.
Tengo que tomar un billete.
Tehn'-goh keh toh-mahr' oon bee-lyeh'-teh.

First class.
Primera clase.
Pree-meh'-rah klah'-seh.

Second class.
Segunda clase.
Seh-goon'-dah klah'-seh.

One way.
Sólo ida.
Soh'-loh ee'-dah.

Round trip.
Ida y vuelta.
Ee'-dah ee vwehl'-tah.

Is there a dining car?
¿Hay un coche comedor?
Ah'-ee oon koh'-cheh koh-meh-dohr'?

Does this train go to . . . ?
¿Va este tren a . . . ?
Vah eh'-steh trehn ah . . . ?

Does this train stop at . . . ?
¿Para este tren en . . . ?
Pah'-rah eh'-steh trehn ehn . . . ?

Is the train late?
¿Está el tren de retraso?
Eh-stah' ehl trehn de reh-trah'-soh?

Is this seat occupied?
¿Está ocupado este asiento?
Eh-stah' oh-koo-pah'-doh eh'-steh ah-syehn'-toh?

What is the name of this station?
¿Cómo se llama esta estación?
Koh'-moh seh lyah'-mah eh'-stah eh-stah-syohn'?

How long do we stop here?
¿Cuánto tiempo paramos aquí?
Kwahn'-toh tyehm-'poh pah-rah'-mohs ah-kee'?

May I open the window?
¿Puedo abrir la ventanilla?
Pweh'-doh ah-breer' lah vehn-tah-nee'-lyah?

Please close the door.
Cierre la portezuela, por favor.
Syeh'-rreh lah pohr-teh-sweh'-lah, pohr fah-vohr'.

I have missed the train!
¡He perdido el tren!
Eh pehr-dee'-doh ehl trehn!

When does the next train leave?
¡Cuándo sale el próximo tren?
Kwahn'-doh sah'-leh ehl prohk'-see-moh trehn?

Where is the waiting room?
¿Dónde está la sala de espera?
Dohn'-deh eh-stah' lah sah'-lah deh eh-speh'-rah?

Where is the lavatory?
¿Dónde está el retrete?
Dohn'-deh eh-stah' ehl reh-treh'-teh?

The train is arriving now.
El tren llega ahora mismo.
Ehl trehn lyeh'-gah ah-oh'-rah mees'-moh.

Tickets, please.
Los billetes, por favor.
Lohs bee-lyeh'-tehs pohr fah-vohr'.

All aboard!
¡Señores viajeros al tren!
Seh-nyoh'-rehs vee-ah-heh'-rohs ahl trehn!

The train is leaving.
El tren sale.
Ehl trehn sah'-leh.

Arrivals.
Llegadas.
Lyeh-gah'-dahs.

Departures.
Salidas.
Sah-lee'-dahs.

Express train.
El tren expreso; el rápido.
Ehl trehn ehs-preh'-soh; ehl rah'-pee-doh.

Local train.
El tren regular.
Ehl trehn reh-goo-lahr'

Getting Around by Ship and Plane

If you go abroad on a ship or airplane, your first chance to use your Spanish will come in transit. Being able to speak with the personnel can be an exciting start to a journey. They will be more helpful, too, if you make an effort to speak to them in their language. And your efforts will be rewarded.

There's the harbor (the port).
Allá está el puerto.
Ah-lyah' eh-stah' ehl pwehr'-toh.

Where is the pier?
¿Dónde está el muelle?
Dohn'-deh eh-stah' ehl mweh'-lyeh?

When does the ship sail?
¿A qué hora sale el buque?
Ah keh oh'-rah sah'-leh ehl boo'-keh?

Let's go on board!
¡Vamos a bordo!
Vah'-mohs ah bohr'-doh!

Where is cabin number . . . ?
¿Dónde está el camarote número . . . ?
Dohn'-deh eh-stah' ehl kah-mah-roh'-teh noo'-meh-roh . . . ?

Is this my cabin (stateroom)?
¿Es éste mi camarote?
Ehs eh'-steh mee kah-mah-roh'-teh?

Steward, do you have the key to my cabin?
¿Camarero, tiene la llave de mi camarote?
Kah-mah-reh'-roh, tyeh'-neh lah lyah'-veh deh mee kah-mah-roh'-teh?

I'm looking for the dining room.
Busco el comedor.
Boos'-koh ehl koh-meh-dohr'.

We want a table for two.
Queremos una mesa para dos.
Keh-reh'-mohs oo'-nah meh'-sah pah'-rah dohs.

A first-class cabin.
Un camarote de primera clase.
Oon kah-meh-roh'-teh deh pree-meh'-rah klah'-seh.

A second-class cabin.
Un camarote de segunda clase.
Oon kah-mah-roh'-teh deh seh-goon'-dah klah'-seh.

Let's go on deck.
Vamos a la cubierta.
Vah'-mohs ah lah koo-byehr'-tah.

I would like a deck chair.
Quisiera una silla de cubierta.
Kee-syeh'-rah oo'-nah see'-lyah deh koo-byehr'-tah.

I would like to eat by the swimming pool.
Quisiera comer cerca de la piscina.
Kee-syeh'-rah koh-mehr' sehr'-kah deh lah pees-see'-nah.

The ship arrives at seven o'clock.
El buque llega a las siete.
Ehl boo'-keh lyeh'-gah ah lahs syeh'-teh.

When do we go ashore?
¿Cuándo nos desembarcamos?
Kwahn'-doh nohs deh-sehm-bahr-kah'-mohs?

Where is the gangplank?
¿Dónde está la plancha?
Dohn'-deh eh-stah' lah plahn'-chah?

The landing card, please.
El permiso de desembarque, por favor.
Ehl pehr-mee'-soh deh deh-sehm-bahr'-keh, pohr fah-vohr'.

I wasn't seasick at all!
¡No tenía mareo de ningún modo!
Noh teh-nee'-ah mah-reh'-oh deh neen-goon' moh'-doh!

Have a good trip!
¡Buen viaje!
Bwehn vee-ah'-heh!

I want to go to the airport.
Quiero ir al aeropuerto.
Kyeh'-roh eer ahl ah-eh-roh-pwehr'-toh.

Drive me to the airport.
Condúzcame al aeropuerto.
Kohn-doos'-kah-meh ahl ah-eh-roh-pwehr'-toh.

When does the plane leave? **When does it arrive?**
¿A qué hora sale el avión? ¿A qué hora llega?
Ah keh oh'-rah sah'-leh ehl *Ah keh oh'-rah lyeh'-gah?*
ah-vyohn'?

Flight number . . . leaves at . . . .
El vuelo número . . . sale a . . . .
Ehl vweh'-loh noo'-meh-roh . . . sah'-leh ah . . . .

From which gate?
¿De qué puerta?
Deh keh pwehr'-tah?

I want to reconfirm my flight.
Quiero reconfirmar mi vuelo.
Kyeh'-roh reh-kohn-feer-mahr' mee vweh'-loh.

Ticket, please.
El billete, por favor.
Ehl bee-leyh'-teh, pohr fah-vohr'.

Boarding pass, please.
El permiso de bordo, por favor.
Ehl pehr-mee'-soh deh bohr'-doh, pohr fah-vohr'.

Please fasten your seat belts.
Fijen los cinturones, por favor.
Fee'-hehn lohs seen-too-roh'-nehs, pohr fah-vohr'.

No smoking.
No fume.
Noh foo'-meh.

Stewardess, a small pillow, please.
Camarera, una almohada pequeña, por favor.
*Kah-mah-reh'-rah, oo'-nah ahl-moh-ah'-dah peh-keh'-nyah,
    pohr fah-vohr'.*

I fly to Europe every year.
Vuelo a Europa todos los años.
Vweh'-loh ah eh-oo-roh'-pah toh'-dohs lohs ah'-nyohs.

The airplane is taking off!
¡El avión despega!
Ehl ah-vyohn' deh-speh'-gah!

Is a meal served during this flight?
¿Se sirve una comida durante este vuelo?
*Seh seer'-veh oo'-nah koh-mee'-dah doo-rahn'-teh eh'-steh
    vweh'-loh?*

The airplane will land in ten minutes.
El avión aterrizará en diez minutos.
Ehl ah-vyohn' ah-teh-rree-sah-rah' ehn dyehs mee-noo'-tohs.

There will be a delay.
Habrá una demora.
Ah-brah' oo'-nah deh-moh'-rah.

There's the runway!
¡Allá está la pista!
Ah-lyah' eh-stah' lah pee'-stah!

We have arrived.
Hemos llegado.
Eh'-mohs lyeh-gah'-doh.

Health

We hope you will never need the phrases you will find in this section; but emergencies do arise, and sickness does overwhelm. Since a physician's diagnosis often depends on what you, the patient, can tell him, you will want to make your woes clearly understood. If you have a chronic medical problem, you might well arrange to have various prescriptions or descriptions of the difficulty in hand or translated before you leave on your trip.

I need a doctor.
Necesito un médico.
Neh-seh-see´-toh oon meh´-dee-koh.

Send for a doctor.
Mande venir un médico.
Mahn´-deh veh-neer´ oon meh´-dee-koh.

Are you the doctor?
¿Es usted el médico?
Ehs oos-tehd´ ehl meh´-dee-koh?

What is the matter with you?
¿Qué tiene usted?
Keh tyeh'-neh oos-tehd'?

I don't feel well.
No me siento bien.
Noh meh syehn'-toh byehn.

I am sick.
Estoy enfermo (*m*)/enferma (*f*).
Eh-stoy' ehn-fehr-'moh (m) /-mah (f).

How long have you been sick?
¿Desde cuánto tiempo está enfermo (*m*) / enferma (*f*)?
*Dehs'-deh kwahn'-toh tyehm'-poh eh-stah' ehn-fehr'-moh
    (m) /-mah(f)?*

I have a headache.
Tengo dolor de cabeza.
Tehn'-goh doh-lohr' deh kah-beh'-sah.

Where is the hospital?
¿Dónde está el hospital?
Dohn'-deh eh-stah' ehl oh-spee-tahl'?

Is there a drugstore near here?
¿Hay una farmacia cerca de aquí?
Ah'-ee oo'-nah fahr-mah'-syah sehr'-kah deh ah-kee'?

I have a stomach ache.
Tengo dolor de estómago.
Tehn'-goh doh-lohr' deh eh-stoh'-mah-goh.

Where does it hurt?
¿Dónde duele?
Dohn'-deh dweh'-leh?

My leg hurts.
Me duele la pierna.
Meh dweh'-leh lah pyehr'-nah.

My finger is bleeding.
Mi dedo sangra.
Mee deh'-doh sahn'-grah.

Do I have a fever?
¿Tengo una fiebre?
Tehn'-goh oo'-nah fyeh'-breh?

I have burned myself.
Me he quemado.
Meh eh keh-mah'-doh.

You must stay in bed.
Usted tiene que guardar cama.
Oos-tehd' tyeh'-neh keh gwahr-dahr' kah-mah.

---

the arm, the arms
el brazo, los brazos
ehl brah'-soh, lohs brah'-sohs

the back
la espalda
lah eh-spahl'-dah

the bladder
la vejiga
lah veh-hee'-gah

the bone
el hueso
ehl weh'-soh

the chest
el pecho
ehl peh'-choh

the ear, the ears
la oreja (el oído), las orejas (los oídos)
lah oh-reh'-hah (ehl oh-ee'-doh), lahs oh-reh'-hahs, (lohs oh-ee'-dohs)

the elbow
el codo
ehl koh'-doh

the eye, the eyes
el ojo, los ojos
ehl oh'-hoh, lohs oh'-hohs

the face
la cara
lah kah'-rah

the finger
el dedo
ehl deh'-doh

the foot, the feet
el pie, los pies
ehl pyeh, lohs pyehs

the forehead
la frente
lah frehn'-teh

How long?
¿Cuánto tiempo?
Kwahn'-toh tyehm'-poh?

At least two days.
Por los menos dos días.
Pohr loh meh'-nohs dohs dee'-ahs.

Show me your tongue.
Muéstreme la lengua.
Mweh'-streh-meh lah lehn'-gwah.

the hair el cabello (el pelo) *ehl kah-beh'-lyoh, ehl peh'-loh*	**my hair** mi cabello, mi pelo *mee kah-beh'-lyoh, mee peh'-loh*
the hand, the hands la mano, las manos *lah mah'-noh, lahs mah'-nohs*	**the leg, the legs** la pierna, las piernas *lah pyehr'-nah, lahs pyehr'-nahs*
the heart el corazón *ehl koh-rah-sohn'*	**the hip** la cadera *lah kah-deh'-rah*
the joint la coyuntura *lah koh-yoon-too'-rah*	**the kidneys** los riñones *lohs ree-nyoh'-nehs*
the knee la rodilla *lah roh-dee'-lyah*	**the head** la cabeza *lah kah-beh'-sah*
the liver el hígado *ehl ee'-gah-doh*	**the lung, the lungs** el pulmón, los pulmones *ehl pool-mohn', lohs pool-moh'-nehs*
the mouth la boca *lah boh'-kah*	**the muscle** el músculo *ehl moos'-koo-loh*

Lie down.
Acuéstese.
Ah-kweh'-steh-seh.

Get up.
Levántese.
Leh-vahn'-teh-seh.

I have a cold.
Tengo un resfriado.
Tehn'-goh oon rehs-free-ah'-doh.

Do you smoke?
¿Fuma usted?
Foo'-mah oos-tehd'?

---

the neck
el cuello
ehl kweh'-lyoh

the nose
la nariz
lah nah-rees'

the shoulder
el hombro
ehl ohm'-broh

the skin
la piel
lah pyehl

the skull
el cráneo
ehl krah'-neh-oh

the spine
el espinazo
ehl eh-spee-nah'-soh

the stomach
el estómago
ehl eh-stoh'-mah-goh

the thigh
el muslo
ehl moos'-loh

the throat
la garganta
lah gahr-gahn'-tah

the thumb
el pulgar
ehl pool-gahr'

the toe
el dedo del pie
ehl deh'-doh dehl pyeh

the tooth, the teeth
el diente, los dientes
ehl dyehn'-teh, lohs dyehn'-tehs

the waist
la cintura
lah seen-too'-rah

the wrist
la muñeca
lah moo-nyeh'-kah

Yes, I smoke.
Sí, fumo.
See, foo'-moh.

No, I don't smoke.
No, no fumo.
Noh, noh foo'-moh.

Do you sleep well?
¿Duerme usted bien?
Dwehr'-meh oos-tehd' byehn?

No, I don't sleep well.
No, no duermo bien.
Noh, noh dwehr'-moh byehn.

I cough frequently.
Toso frecuentemente.
Toh'-soh freh-kwehn-teh-mehn'-teh.

Take this medicine three times a day.
Tome esta medicina tres veces por día.
*Toh'-meh eh'-stah meh-dee-see'-nah trehs veh'-sehs pohr
dee'-ah.*

Here is a prescription.
He aquí una receta.
Eh ah-kee' oo'-nah reh-seh'-tah.

Can you come again tomorrow?
¿Puede usted venir otra vez mañana?
*Pweh'-deh oos-tehd' veh-neer' oh'-trah vehs mah-nyah'-
nah?*

Yes, I can come.
Sí, puedo venir.
See, pweh'-doh veh-neer'.

I will come later.
Vendré más tarde.
Vehn-dreh' mahs tahr'-deh.

He's a good doctor.
Él es un buen médico.
Ehl ehs oon bwehn meh'-dee-koh.

Sightseeing

No phrase book can possibly supply you with all the phrases you might want in the infinite number of situations, emotions, likes, and dislikes you will encounter in your travels. The basics are here, but they can only be a beginning. The dictionary at the back of this book will supply you with a larger vocabulary to use with the phrases given here. In addition, local bilingual or multilingual guides are usually very helpful in supplying other language information concerning a given situation. If an unusual phrase is required, ask him and it will be given to you gladly.

I would like to go sightseeing.
Quisiera ver los puntos de interés.
Kee-syeh'-rah vehr lohs poon'-tohs deh een-teh-rehs'.

How long does the tour last?
¿Cuánto tiempo dura la excursión?
Kwahn'-toh tyehm'-poh doo'-rah lah ehs-koor-syohn'?

It lasts three hours.
Dura tres horas.
Doo'-rah trehs oh'-rahs.

Are you the guide?
¿Es usted el guía?
Ehs oos-tehd' ehl gee'-ah?

What is the name of this place?
¿Cómo se llama este lugar?
Koh'-moh seh lyah'-mah eh'-steh loo-gahr'?

Are the museums open today?
¿Están abiertos los museos hoy?
Eh-stahn' ah-byehr'-tohs lohs moo-seh'-ohs oy?

No, the museums are closed today.
No, los museos están cerrados hoy.
Noh, lohs moo-seh'-ohs eh-stahn' seh-rrah'-dohs oy.

The stores are open.
Las tiendas están abiertas.
Lahs tyehn'-dahs eh-stahn' ah-byehr'-tahs.

I would like to visit an art museum.
Quisiera visitar un museo de arte.
Kee-syeh'-rah vee-see-tahr' oon moo-seh'-oh deh ahr'-teh.

Is there an exhibition there now?
¿Hay una exposición allá ahora?
Ah'-ee oo'-nah ehs-poh-see-syohn' ah-lyah' ah-oh'-rah?

I would like to see the city.
Quisiera ver la ciudad.
Kee-syeh'-rah vehr lah syoo-dahd'.

What is the name of that church?
¿Cómo se llama esa iglesia?
Koh'-moh seh lyah'-mah eh'-sah ee-gleh'-see-ah?

May we go in?
¿Podemos entrar?
Poh-deh'-mohs ehn-trahr'?

Is the old church closed this morning?
¿Está cerrada esta mañana la iglesia vieja?
Eh-stah' seh-rrah'-dah eh'-stah mah-nyah'-nah lah ee-gleh'-see-ah vyeh'-hah?

Will it be open this evening?
¿Se abrirá esta tarde?
eh ah-bree-rah' eh'-stah tahr'-deh?

This is the main square of the city.
Ésta es la plaza principal de la ciudad.
Eh'-stah ehs lah plah'-sah preen-see-pahl' deh lah syoo-dahd'.

May I take pictures here?
¿Puedo sacar fotografías aquí?
Pweh'-doh sah-kahr' foh-toh-grah-fee'-ahs ah-kee'?

We have walked a lot.
Hemos caminado mucho.
Eh'-mohs kah-mee-nah'-doh moo'-choh.

I am tired.
Estoy cansado (*m*)/cansada (*f*).
Eh-stoy' kahn-sah'-doh (m)/-dah (f).

Let's sit down.
Sentémonos.
Sehn-teh'-moh-nohs.

Where does this street lead to?
¿Por dónde va esta calle?
Pohr dohn'-deh vah eh'-stah kah'-lyeh?

To the cathedral.
A la catedral.
Ah lah kah-teh-drahl'.

What is that monument?
¿Qué es ese monumento?
Keh ehs eh'-seh moh-noo-mehn'-toh?

Is that a theater?
¿Es ése un teatro?
Ehs eh'-seh oon teh-ah'-troh?

It's a movie house.
Ése es un cine.
Eh'-seh ehs oon see'-neh.

What is the name of this park?
¿Cómo se llama este parque?
Koh'-moh seh lyah'-mah eh'-steh pahr'-keh?

We cross the street here.
Atravesamos la calle aquí.
Ah-trah-veh-sah'-mohs lah kah'-lyeh ah-kee'.

Will we visit a castle?
¿Visitaremos un castillo?
Vee-see-tah-reh'-mohs oon kahs-tee'-lyoh?

We will visit a palace.
Visitaremos un palacio.
Vee-see-tah-reh'-mohs oon pah-lah'-syoh.

Who lives in this palace?
¿Quién vive en este palacio?
Kyehn vee'-veh ehn eh'-steh pah-lah'-syoh?

Nobody lives here.
Nadie vive aquí.
Nah'-dyeh vee'-veh ah-kee'.

What is the name of this river?
¿Cómo se llama este río?
Koh'-moh seh lyah'-mah eh'-steh ree'-oh?

This is the longest bridge in the city.
Éste es el puente más largo de la ciudad.
Eh'-steh ehs ehl pwehn'-teh mahs lahr'-goh deh lah syoo-dahd'.

There's too much water in the boat.
Hay demasiada agua en el barco.
Ah'-ee deh-mah-syah'-dah ah'-gwah ehn ehl bahr'-koh.

Is our hotel near the river?
¿Está nuestro hotel cerca del río?
Eh-stah' nwehs'-troh oh-tehl' sehr'-kah dehl ree'-oh?

This is the shopping center.
Éste es el centro de compras.
Eh'-steh ehs ehl sehn'-troh deh kohm'-prahs.

Is it far from here to the beach?
¿Está lejos de aquí a la playa?
Eh-stah' leh'-hohs deh ah-kee' ah lah plah'-yah?

I would like to go swimming this morning.
Quisiera ir a nadar esta mañana.
Kee-syeh'-rah eer ah nah-dahr' eh'-stah mah-nyah'-nah.

If it doesn't rain, we'll go there.
Si no llueve, iremos allá.
See noh lyweh'-veh, ee-reh'-mohs ah-lyah'.

Thank you for an interesting tour.
Le agradezco de una excursión interesante.
Leh ah-grah-dehs'-koh deh oo'-nah ehs-koor-syohn' een-teh-reh-sahn'-teh.

Thank you very much for it.
Se la agradezco mucho.
Seh lah ah-grah-dehs'-koh moo'-choh.

I like it.	**I liked it.**
Me agrada.	Me agradó.
Meh ah-grah'-dah.	*Meh ah-grah-doh'.*

DICTIONARY

Some Tips on Spanish Grammar

Gender Nouns in Spanish are either masculine or feminine. This is important to know since the form of other parts of speech (articles, adjectives, pronouns) depends on whether they modify or appear in connection with a masculine or feminine noun. The indefinite and definite articles and adjectives always agree with the noun in number and gender.

As a rule, nouns ending in "o" are masculine and those ending in "a" are feminine. Nouns ending in "e" may be either masculine or feminine and the correct gender must be learned when the word is first encountered.

The definite article (*the*) is *el* for masculine singular nouns and feminine singular nouns beginning with accented "a," and *la* for feminine singular nouns not beginning with accented "a." Plural masculine nouns take the definite article *los* and plural feminine nouns take the definite article *las*. Notice the following:

el río (the river)   los ríos (the rivers)
el agua (the water)
la casa (the house)   las casas (the houses)

The indefinite articles (*a, an*) are *un* for masculine singular nouns and *una* for feminine singular.

Adjectives vary in genber according to the nouns they modify. Notice the following:

un río larg*o*(a long river) ríos larg*os* (long rivers)
una playa larg*a*   playas larg*as*
  (a long beach)   (long beaches)

When a girl or women speaks of herself or refers to another female, the feminine form of the adjective must be used:

Estoy enfermo.	**I am sick.** (a man speaking)
Estoy enferma.	**I am sick.** (a woman speaking)
Está enfermo.	**He is sick.**
Está enferma.	**She is sick.**
Están enfermos.	**They are sick.** (men or men and women)
Están enfermas.	**They are sick.** (women only)

Plurals The plurals of nouns and adjectives are formed by adding *-s* to words ending in a vowel and by adding *-es* to words ending in a consonant.

manzana (apple)	manzanas (apples)
diente (tooth)	dientes (teeth)
libro (book)	libros (books)
corazón (heart)	corazones (hearts)
lápiz (pencil)	lápices (pencils)

Word Order The order of words in Spanish sentences is much the same as in English, with two prime exceptions. In Spanish the adjective usually follows the noun:

un río largo	**a long river**
ríos largos	**long rivers**
una playa larga	**a long beach**
playas largas	**long beaches**

And the indirect and direct object pronouns, in an affirmative statement, precedes the verb:

He gave me the money.	Me dió el dinero
He gave it to me.	Me lo dió

Verbs Person is indicated in Spanish verbs by endings attached to the verb stem. In regular verbs, the verb stem is got by dropping the *-ar*, *-er*, or *-ir* from the infinitive form. (Some verb stems are irregular.) Notice the following:

hablar, **to speak**
habl*o*, **I speak**
habl*a*, **he, she speaks; you** (polite) **speak**
habl*amos*, **we speak**
habl*an*, **they speak; you** (pl., polite) **speak**

perder, **to lose**
pierd*o*, **I lose**
pierd*e*, **he, she loses; you** (polite) **lose**
perd*emos*, **we lose**
pierd*en*, **they lose; you** (pl., polite) **lose**

salir, **to go out**
salg*o*, **I go out**
sal*e*, **he, she goes out; you** (polite) **go out**
sal*imos*, **we go out**
sal*en*, **they go out; you** (pl., polite) **go out**

There is a set of personal pronouns that indicate person, but they are used largely for emphasis:

hablo, I speak   yo hablo, *I* speak
hablé, I spoke   yo hablé, *I* spoke

The reflexive pronouns used with reflexive verbs (those ending in *-se* in the Dictionary) follow the same rule for word order given above.

a, un, una *oon, oo'-nah*
able: to be able, poder *poh-dehr'*
aboard, a bordo *ah bohr'-doh*
about *adv.,* casi *kah'-see*
about *prep.,* sobre *soh'-breh*
above, arriba *ah-rree'-bah*
abroad, al extranjero *al eh-strahn-heh'-roh*
absolutely, absolutamente *ahb-soh-loo-tah-mehn'-teh*
accelerate, acelerar *ah-seh-leh-rahr'*
accelerator, acelerador (m) *ah-seh-leh-rah-dohr'*
accent *n.,* acento *ah-sehn'-toh*
accept, aceptar *ah-sehp-tahr'*
accident, accidente (m) *ahk-see-dehn'-teh* [15]
according to, según *seh-goon'*
account *n.,* cuenta *kwehn'-tah*
ache *n.,* dolor (m) *doh-lohr'* [95]
ache *v.,* doler *doh-lehr'*
acquaintance, conocimiento *koh-noh-see-myehn'-toh*
across, a través *ah trah-vehs'*
act *n.,* acto *ahk'-toh*
act [do], hacer *ah-sehr';* [drama], representar *reh-preh-sehn-tahr'*
active, activo *ahk-tee'-voh*
actor, actor *ahk-tohr'*
actress, actriz *ahk-trees'*
actual, verdadero *vehr-dah-deh'-roh*
add, sumar *soo-mahr'*
address *n.,* dirección (f) *dee-rehk-syohn'* [31]
admiration, admiración *ahd-mee-rah-syohn'*
admire, admirar *ahd-mee-rahr'*
admission, admisión *ahd-mee-syohn'*
admit, admitir *ahd-mee-teer'*
adorable, adorable *ah-doh-rah'-bleh*
advance *v.,* avanzar *ah-vahn-sahr'*
advantage, ventaja *vehn-tah'-hah*
adventure, aventura *ah-vehn-too'-rah*

advertisement, anuncio *ah-noon'-syoh*
advice, consejo *kohn-seh'-hoh*
advise, consejar *kohn-seh-hahr'*
affectionate, afectuoso *ah-fehk-twoh'-soh*
afraid: to be afraid, tener miedo de *teh-nehr' myeh'-doh deh* [7]
after, después *dehs-pwehs'*
afternoon, tarde *tahr'-deh*
afterwards, después *dehs-pwehs'*
again, otra vez *oh'-trah vehs*
against, contra *kohn'-trah*
age, edad (f) *eh-dahd'*
agent, agente (m) *ah-hehn'-teh*
ago, hace *ah'-seh*
agree: to be in accord, estar de acuerdo *ehs-tahr' deh ah-kwehr'-doh*
agreeable [pleasing], agradable *ah-grah-dah'-bleh*
agreement, acuerdo *ah-kwehr'-doh*
ahead: straight ahead, todo seguido *toh'-doh seh-gee'-doh*
air, aire (m) *ah'-ee-reh* [77]
air filter, filtro de aire *feel'-troh deh ah'-ee-reh*
air line, línea aérea *lee'-neh-ah ah-eh'-reh-ah*
airmail, correo aéreo *koh-rreh'-oh ah-eh'-reh-oh*
airplane, avión *ah-vee-yohn'* [92, 93]
airport, aeropuerto *ah-eh-roh-pwehr'-toh* [47, 91]
alarm, alarma *ah-lahr'-mah*
alarm clock, despertador (m) *dehs-pehr-tah-dohr'*
alcohol, alcohol (m) *ahl-koh-ohl'*
alike, semejante, parecido *seh-meh-hahn'-teh, pah-reh-see'-doh*
alive, vivo *vee'-voh*
all, todo *toh-doh* **not at all** [none], nada *nah'-dah;* [it's nothing], no hay de qué *noh ah'-ee deh keh* **after all,** después de todo *dehs-pwehs' deh toh'-doh*
allergy, alergia *ah-lehr'-hia*
allow, permitir *pehr-mee-teer'*

almond, almendra *ahl-mehn'-drah*

almost, casi *kah'-see*

alone, solo *soh'-loh*

along, a lo largo de *ah loh lahr'-goh deh*

already, ya *yah* [59]

also, también *tahm-byehn'*

altar, altar (m) *ahl-tahr'*

alter, alterar *ahl-teh-rahr'*

alteration [of clothing], arreglo *ah-rreh'-gloh*

although, aunque *ah-oon'-keh*

altogether, enteramente *ehn-teh-rah-mehn'-teh*

always, siempre *syehm'-preh*

am: I am, soy, estoy *soy, ehs-toy'*

ambassador, embajador *ehm-bah-hah-dohr'*

American, americano *ah-meh-ree-kah'-noh*

amount, cantidad (f) *kahn-tee-dahd'*

amusement, diversión (f) *dee-vehr-syohn'*

amusing, divertido *dee-vehr-tee'-doh*

an, un, una *oon, oo'-nah*

and, y, e *ee, eh*

anger *n.,* enojo *eh-noh'-hoh*

angry, enojado *eh-noh-hah'-doh*

animal, animal *ah-nee-mahl'*

ankle, tobillo *toh-bee'-lyoh*

announce, anunciar *ah-nuhn-syahr'*

annoy, molestar *moh-lehs-tahr'*

another, otro *oh'-troh*

answer *n.,* contestación (f), respuesta *kohn-tehs-tah-syohn', rehs-pwehs'-tah*

answer *v.,* responder, contestar *rehs-pohn-dehr', kohn-teh-stahr'* [45]

antique shop, tienda de antigüedades *tyehn'-dah deh ahn-tee-gweh-dah'-dehs*

anxious, ansioso *ahn-syoh'-soh*

any, cualquier *kwahl-kyehr'*

anyone, alguien *ahl'-gyehn*

anyhow, de todos modos *deh toh'-dohs moh'-dohs*
anything, algo *ahl'-goh*
anywhere, dondequiera *dohn-deh-kyeh'-rah*
apartment, apartamiento *ah-pahr-tah-myehn'-toh*
apologize, excusarse *ehs-koo-sahr'-seh*
apology, excusa *ehs-koo'-sah*
appear, aparecer *ah-pah-reh-sehr'*
appendicitis, apendicitis *ah-pehn-dee-see'-tees*
appendix, apéndice (m) *ah-pehn'-dee-seh*
appetite, apetito *ah-peh-tee'-toh*
appetizer, aperitivo *ah-peh-ree-tee'-voh*
apple, manzana *mahn-sah'-nah*
appointment, cita *see'-tah*
appreciate, apreciar *ah-preh-syahr'*
approve, aprobar *ah-proh-bahr'*
approximately, aproximadamente *ah-prohk-see-mah-dah-mehn'-teh*
April, abril *ah-breel'*
arch, arco *ahr'-koh*
architect, arquitecto *ahr-kee-tehk'-toh*
architecture, arquitectura *ahr-kee-tehk-too'-rah*
are: you are, es, está *ehs, ehs-tah'* **you (pl), they are,** son, están *sohn, ehs-tahn'* **we are,** somos, estamos *soh'-mohs, ehs-tah'-mohs*
area, superficie (f) *soo-pehr-fee'-syeh*
argue, disputar *dees-poo-tahr'*
arm, brazo *brah'-soh*
around, alrededor *ahl-reh-deh-dohr'*
arrange, arreglar *ah-rreh-glahr'*
arrest *v.*, arrestar *ah-rrehs-tahr'*
arrival, llegada *lyeh-gah'-dah* [88]
arrive, llegar *lyeh-gahr'* [26, 48, 88, 91, 93]
art, arte (m) *ahr-teh'* [101]
artichoke, alcachofa *ahl-kah-choh'-fah*
article, artículo *ahr-tee'-koo-loh*
artificial, artificial *ahr-tee-fee-syahl'*

artist, artista (m) *ahr-tees'-tah*
as, como *koh'-moh;* **as well,** también *tahm-byehn'*
ashamed, avergonzado *ah-vehr-gohn-sah'-doh*
ashore, en tierra, a tierra *ehn-tyeh'-rrah, ah tyeh'-rrah;*
  go ashore, desembarcar *dehs-ehm-bahr-kahr'* [91]
ashtray, cenicero *seh-nee-seh'-roh* [52]
ask, preguntar *preh-goon-tahr'*
asleep, dormido *dohr-mee'-doh* **to fall asleep,** dormirse
  dohr-meer'-seh
asparagus, espárrago *ehs-pah'-rrah-goh*
aspirin, aspirina *ahs-pee-ree'-nah*
assist, ayudar *ah-yoo-dahr'*
assistant, asistente (m) *ah-sees-tehn'-teh*
associate *n.,* asociado *ah-soh-syah'-doh*
association, asociación (f) *ah-soh-syah-syohn'*
assure, asegurar *ah-seh-goo-rahr'*
at *prep.,* en, a *ehn, ah*
Atlantic, Atlántico *aht-lahn'-tee-koh*
attach, juntar *hoon-tahr'*
attain [reach], alcanzar *ahl-kahn-sahr'*
attempt *v.,* probar *proh-bahr'*
attend, asistir a *ah-sees-teer' ah*
attention, atención (f) *ah-tehn-syohn'*
attract, atraer *ah-trah-ehr'*
audience, público *poo'-blee-koh*
August, agosto *ah-gohs'-toh*
aunt, tía *tee'-yah*
author, autor *ow-tohr'*
authority, autoridad (f) *ow-toh-ree-dahd'*
automobile, automóvil (m) *ow-toh-moh'-veel*
autumn, otoño *oh-toh'-nyoh*
available, disponible *dees-poh-nee'-bleh*
avenue, avenida *ah-veh-nee'-dah*
avoid, evitar *eh-vee-tahr'*
await, esperar *ehs-peh-rahr'*
awake *adj.,* despierto *dehs-pyehr'-toh*

awake *v.*, despertar *dehs-pehr-tahr'*
away, fuera, ausente *fweh'-rah, ow-sehn'-teh*
axle, eje (m) *eh'-heh*

baby, nene *neh'-neh*
bachelor, soltero *sohl-teh'-roh*
back *adv.*, atrás *ah-trahs'* **to go back**, remontarse *reh-mohn-tahr'-seh*
back *n.*, espalda *ehs-pahl'-dah*
bacon, tocino *toh-see'-noh*
bad, malo *mah'-loh*
badly, mal *mahl*
bag, saco *sah'-koh*; [suitcase], maleta *mah-leh'-tah* [35, 86]
baggage, equipaje (m) *eh-kee-pah'-heh* [87]
baggage check, contraseña, talón *kohn-trah-seh'-nyah, tah-lohn'* [87]
bakery, panadería *pah-nah-deh-ree'-yah*
balcony, balcón (m) *bahl-kohn'*
ball, pelota *peh-loh'-tah*
banana, plátano *plah'-tah-noh*
band [music], banda *bahn'-dah*
bandage, vendaje (m) *vehn-dah'-heh*
bank, banco *bahn'-koh* [31]
bar, bar (m) *bahr*
barber, barbero *bahr-beh'-roh*
bargain *n.*, ganga *gahn'-gah*
basket, canasta *kah-nahs'-tah*
bath, baño *bah'-nyoh* [38]
bathe, bañarse *bah-nyahr'-seh*
bathing suit, traje de baño *trah'-heh deh bah'-nyoh*
bathroom, cuarto de baño *kwahr'-toh deh bah'-nyoh* [40]
battery, batería *bah-teh-ree'-yah*
bay, bahía *bah-ee'-yah*
be: to be, ser, estar *sehr, ehs-tahr'*
beach, playa *plah'-yah* [104]

bean, habichuela, fava, frijole *ah-bee-chweh'-lah, fah'-vah, free-hoh'-leh*
beard, barba *bahr'-bah*
beautiful, hermoso *ehr-moh'-soh* [10]
beauty parlor, salón de belleza (m) *sah-lohn' deh beh-lyeh'-sah*
because, porque *pohr'-keh*
become, ponerse *poh-nehr'-seh*
bed, cama *kah'-mah* [96]   **to go to bed,** acostarse *ah-koh-stahr'-seh*
bedroom, dormitorio *dohr-mee-toh'-ryoh*
bee, abeja *ah-beh'-hah*
beef, carne de res (m) *kahr'-neh deh rehs*
beefsteak, biftec (m) *beef'-tehk*
beer, cerveza *sehr-veh'-sah* [58]
beet, remolacha *reh-moh-lah'-chah*
before [time], antes *ahn'-tehs*
before [place], delante *deh-lahn'-teh*
begin, empezar *ehm-peh-sahr'*
beginning, principio *preen-see'-pyoh*
behind, detrás *deh-trahs'*
believe, creer *kreh-yehr'*
bell, campana *kahm-pah'-nah*
belong, pertenecer *pehr-teh-neh-sehr'*
belt, cinturón (m) *seen-too-rohn'* [76, 92]
beside, al lado (de) *ahl lah'-doh (deh)*
besides, además *ah-deh-mahs'*
best, el mejor, la mejor *ehl meh-hohr', lah meh-hohr'*
better, mejor *meh-hohr'*
between, entre *ehn-treh'*
big, grande *grahn'-deh* [72]
bill, cuenta *kwehn'-tah* [59, 73]
bird, pájaro *pah'-hah-roh*
birth, nacimiento *nah-see-myehn'-toh*
birthday, cumpleaños (m, pl) *koom-pleh-ah'-nyohs*
bit: a bit, poquito *poh-kee'-toh*

bite *v.*, morder *mohr-dehr'*
black, negro *neh'-groh* [70]
blanket, frazada *frah-sah'-dah*
bleed, sangrar *sahn-grahr'* [95]
blind, ciego *syeh'-goh*
blister, ampolla *ahm-poh'-lyah*
block *n.*, cuadra *kwah'-drah*
blonde, rubio *roo'-byoh*
blood, sangre (f) *sahn'-greh*
blouse, blusa *bloo'-sah*
blue, azul *ah-sool'* [70]
board: room and board, pensión *pehn-syohn'*
boarding house, pensión (f) *pehn-syohn'*
boarding pass, permiso de bordo *pehr-mee'-soh deh bohr'-doh* [92]
boat, barco *bahr'-koh*
body, cuerpo *kwehr'-poh*
boil *v.*, hervir *ehr-veer'*
bone, hueso *weh'-soh*
book, libro *lee'-broh*
bookstore, librería *lee-breh-ree'-yah*
booth, cabina telefónica *kah-bee'-nah teh-leh-foh'-nee-kah*
boot, bota *boh'-tah*
border *n.*, frontera *frohn-teh'-rah*
born: to be born, nacer *nah-sehr'*
borrow, pedir prestado *peh-deer' prehs-tah'-doh*
both, ambos *ahm-bohs*
bottle, botella *boh-teh'-lyah* [58] **bottle opener,** abre botellas (m) *ah'-breh boh-teh'-lyahs*
bottom, fondo *fohn'-doh*
box, caja *kah'-hah* [35]
boy, muchacho *moo-chah'-choh*
bracelet, pulsera *pool-seh'-rah*
brake *n.*, freno *freh'-noh*
brandy, aguardiente (m) *ah'-gwahr-dyehn'-teh*
brassiere, sostén (m) *sohs-tehn'*

brave, valiente *vah-lyehn'-teh*
bread, pan (m) *pahn*
break *v.*, romper *rohm-pehr'*
breakfast, desayuno *deh-sah-yoo'-noh* [39, 51, 52, 54]
breast, pecho *peh'-choh*
breath, respiración (f) *reh-spee-rah-syohn'*
breathe, respirar *reh-spee-rahr'*
bridge, puente (m) *pwehn'-teh* [103]
bright, claro *klah'-roh*
bring, traer *trah-ehr'* [13, 52, 54, 57, 58]
broken, roto *roh'-toh*
brother, hermano *ehr-mah'-noh* [3]
brown, pardo *pahr'-doh* [70]
bruise *n.*, contusión (f) *kohn-too-syohn'*
brush *n.*, cepillo *seh-pee'-lyoh*
brunette, moreno, morena *moh-reh'-noh, moh-reh'-nah*
build *v.*, construir *kohn-stroo-eer'*
building, edificio *eh-dee-fee'-syoh*
bull, toro *toh'-roh*
bullfight, corrida de toros *koh-rree'-dah deh toh'-rohs*
burn *n.*, quemadura *keh-mah-doo'-rah*
burn *v.*, quemar *keh-mahr'* [96]
burst *v.*, reventar *reh-vehn-tahr'*
bus, autobús (m) *ow-toh-boos'* [16, 48, 49]
business, negocios (m) *neh-goh'-syohs*
busy, ocupado *oh-koo-pah'-doh* [45]
but, pero, sino *peh'-roh, see'-noh*
butter, mántequilla, manteca *mahn-teh-kee'-lyah, mahn-teh'-kah* [52, 55]
button, botón (m) *boh-tohn'*
buy, comprar *kohm-prahr'* [68, 69]
by, por *pohr*

cabbage, col (f) *kohl*
cabin, camarote (m), cabina *kah-mah-roh'-teh, kah-bee'-nah* [90]

café, café *kah-feh'*
cake, torta *tohr'-tah*
call *n.,* llamada *lyah-mah'-dah* [44]
call *v.,* llamar *lyah-mahr'* [16, 41, 46]
camera, cámara *kah'-mah-rah*
can *n.,* lata *lah'-tah*
can: to be able, poder *poh-dehr'* **I can,** yo puedo *yoh pweh'-doh*
canal, canal (m) *kah-nahl'*
cancel *v.,* cancelar *kahn-seh-lahr'*
candy, bombones (m) *bohm-boh'-nehs*
candy store, confitería *kohn-fee-teh-ree'-yah*
capital, capital (f) *cah-pee-tahl'*
car, coche (m) *koh'-cheh* [73, 76, 77, 79]
carburetor, carburador (m) *kahr-boo-rah-dohr'*
card, tarjeta *tahr-heh'-tah* [40]
care *n.,* cuidado *kwee-dah'-doh*
care *v.,* curar de *koo-rahr' deh*
careful, cuidadoso *kwee-dah-doh'-soh*
Caribbean, Caribe *kah-ree'-beh*
carpet, alfombra *ahl-fohm'-brah*
carrot, zanahoria *sah-nah-oh'-ree-yah*
carry, llevar *lyeh-vahr'* [36]
cash *n.,* dinero efectivo *dee-neh'-roh eh-fehk-tee'-voh*
cashier, cajero, caja *kah-heh'-roh, kah'-hah* [59]
castanets, castañuelas *kahs-tah-nyoo-eh'-lahs*
Castilian, castellano *kahs-teh-lyah'-noh*
castle, castillo *kahs-tee'-lyoh* [103]
cat, gato *gah'-toh*
catch, coger *koh-hehr'*
cathedral, catedral (f) *kah-teh-drahl'* [102]
Catholic, católico *kah-toh'-lee-koh*
catsup, salsa de tomate *sahl'-sah deh toh-mah'-teh*
cattle, ganado *gah-nah'-doh*
cauliflower, coliflor (f) *koh-lee-flohr'*
caution, cuidado *kwee-dah'-doh*

ceiling, techo *teh'-choh*
celery, apio *ah'-pyoh*
cellar, sótano *soh'-tah-noh*
cemetery, cementerio *seh-mehn-teh'-ryoh*
center, centro *sehn'-troh*
centimeter, centímetro *sehn-tee'-meh-troh*
century, siglo *seeg'-loh*
ceremony, ceremonia *seh-reh-moh'-nyah*
certain, cierto *syehr'-toh*
certainly [gladly], con mucho gusto *kohn moo'-choh goo'-stoh*
chair, silla *see'-lyah*
chambermaid, camarera *kah-mah-reh'-rah* [41]
champagne, champaña *chahm-pah'-nyah*
chance *n.,* oportunidad *oh-pohr-too-nee-dahd'*
change [coins], cambio, suelta *kahm'-byoh, swehl'-tah* [32]
change *v.,* cambiar *kahm-byahr'* [32, 33]
chapel, capilla *kah-pee'-lyah*
charge *v.,* cargar *kahr-gahr'*
charming, encantador *ehn-kahn-tah-dohr'*
chauffeur, chofer (m) *choh'-fehr*
cheap, barato *bah-rah'-toh* [70]
check *n.,* cheque (m) *cheh'-keh* [32] **traveler's check,** cheque de viajeros *cheh'-keh deh vyah-heh'-rohs* [32]
check [one's baggage] *v.,* facturar *fahk-too-rahr'* [86]
check [inspect] *v.,* revisar, inspeccionar *reh-vee-sahr', een-spehk-syoh-nahr'* [79]
cheek, mejilla *meh-hee'-lyah*
cheese, queso *keh'-soh*
cherry, cereza *seh-reh'-sah*
chest, pecho *peh'-choh*
chicken, pollo *poh'-lyoh*
child, niño, niña *nee'-nyoh, nee'-nyah*
chin, barba, barbilla *bahr'-bah, bahr-bee'-lyah*
chocolate, chocolate (m) *choh-koh-lah'-teh*
choose, escoger *ehs-koh-hehr'*

chop, costilla *koh-stee'-lyah*

Christmas, Pascuas de Navidad *pahs'-kwahs deh nah-vee-dahd'*

church, iglesia *ee-gleh'-see-yah* [101, 102]

cigar, puro *poo'-roh*

cigarette, cigarrillo *see-gah-rree'-lyoh* [35, 72]

cinema, cine (m) *see'-neh*

circle, círculo *seer'-koo-loh*

citizen, ciudadano *syoo-dah-dah'-noh*

city, ciudad (f) *syoo-dahd'* [101, 102, 103]

class, clase (f) *klah'-seh* **first class,** primera clase *pree-meh'-rah klah'-seh* **second class,** segunda clase *seh-goon'-dah klah'-seh*

classify, clasificar *klah-see-fee-kahr'*

clean *adj.*, limpio *leem'-pyoh* [41, 57, 59]

clean *v.*, limpiar *leem-pyahr'*

cleaners, tintorería *teen-toh-reh-ree'-yah*

clear, claro *klah'-roh*

climb, subir *soo-beer'*

clock, reloj (m) *reh-lohkh'*

close [near], cerca *sehr'-kah*

close *v.*, cerrar *seh-rrahr'* [35, 41, 64, 87]

closed, cerrado *seh-rrah'-doh* [101, 102]

closet, armario *ahr-mah'-ryoh*

cloth, tela *teh'-lah*

clothes, vestidos (m, pl) *vehs-tee'-dohs*

cloud, nube (f) *noo'-beh* [7]

clutch [of a car], embrague (m) *ehm-brah'-geh*

coast, costa *kohs'-tah*

coat [topcoat], abrigo *ah-bree'-goh;* [suitcoat] saco *sah'-koh*

cockfight, pelea de gallos *peh-leh'-yah deh gah'-lyohs*

cocktail, coctel *kohk-tehl'*

coffee, café (m) *kah-feh'* [52, 54, 55]

cognac, coñac (m) *koh-nyahk'*

coin, moneda *moh-neh'-dah* [45]

cold *adj.*, frío *free'-yoh* [54]   **I am cold,** tengo frío *tehn'-goh free'-yoh*   **it is cold,** hace frío *ah'-seh free'-yoh*
cold *n.*, resfriado, catarro *rehs-free-ah'-doh, kah-tah'-rroh* [98]
collar, cuello *kweh'-lyoh*
collect, cobrar *koh-brahr'*
collection, colección *koh-lehk-syohn'*
college, universidad (f) *oo-nee-vehr-see-dahd'*
collide, chocar *choh-kahr'*
color, color (m) *koh-lohr'* [70]
comb, peine *peh'-ee-neh*
come, venir *veh-neer'* [14, 99]
comfortable, cómodo *koh'-moh-doh*
company, compañía *kohm-pah-nyee'-yah*
comparison, comparación (f) *kohm-pah-rah-syohn'*
compartment, compartimiento *kohm-pahr-tee-myehn'-toh*
complain, quejarse *keh-hahr'-seh*
complete *adj.*, completo *kohm-pleh'-toh*
compliment *n.*, *complido koom-plee'-doh*
concert, concierto *kohn-syehr'-toh*
condition, condición (f) *kohn-dee-syohn'*
confuse, confusar *kohn-foo-sahr'*
congratulations, felicitaciones *feh-lee-see-tah-syohn'-ehs*
connect, conectar *kohn-ehk-tahr'*
consent *v.*, consentir *kohn-sehn-teer'*
consider, considerar *kohn-see-deh-rahr'*
constipated, estreñido *ehs-treh-nyee'-doh*
consul, cónsul *kohn'-sool*
consulate, consulado *kohn-soo-lah'-doh*
contagious, contagioso *kohn-tah-hee-oh'-soh*
contain, contener *kohn-teh-nehr'*
contented, contento *kohn-tehn'-toh*
continue, continuar *kohn-tee-noo-ahr'*
contrary, obstinado *ohb-stee-nah'-doh*   **on the contrary,** al contrario *ahl kohn-trah'-ryoh*
convenient, conveniente *kohn-veh-nyehn'-teh*

conversation, conversación *kohn-vehr-sah-syohn'*

cook *n.*, cocinero *koh-see-neh'-roh*

cook *v.*, cocinar *koh-see-nahr'*

cool, fresco *frehs'-koh* [8]

copy, copia *koh'-pyah*

corkscrew, tirabuzón (m) *tee-rah-boo-sohn'*

corn, maíz (m) *mah-ees'*

corner, esquina *ehs-kee'-nah*

correct *adj.*, correcto *koh-rrehk'-toh*

cost *n.*, costo *kohs'-toh*

cost *v.*, costar *kohs-tahr'* [69, 75]

cotton, algodón (m) *ahl-goh-dohn'*

cough *n.*, tos (f) *tohs*

cough *v.*, toser *toh-sehr'* [99]

count *v.*, contar *kohn-tahr'* [33]

country, país (m), campo *pah-ees'*, *kahm'-poh* [76]

courage, valor (m) *vah-lohr'*

course, curso *koor'-soh* **of course**, naturalmente *nah-too-rahl-mehn'-teh* **main course**, plato principal *plah'-toh preen-see-pahl'*

court, tribunal (m) *tree-boo-nahl'*

court [yard], patio *pah'-tyoh* [39]

cover *v.*, cubrir *koo-breer'*

cow, vaca *vah'-kah*

crab, cangrejo *kahn-greh'-hoh*

cramp, calambre (f) *kah-lahm'-breh*

crazy, loco *loh'-koh*

cream, crema *kreh'-mah;* [for coffee], nata *nah'-tah*

cross *n.*, cruz (f) *kroos*

cross *v.*, cruzar, atravesar *kroo-sahr' ah-trah-veh-sahr'* [103]

crossing, travesía *trah-veh-see'-yah*

crossroads, encrucijada *ehn-kroo-see-hah'-dah*

crowd, muchedumbre (f), gentío *mooch-eh-doom'-breh, hehn-tee'-yoh*

cry *v.*, llorar *lyoh-rahr'*

cucumber, pepino *peh-pee'-noh*

cup, taza *tah'-sah* [55]
curve, curva *koor'-vah*
custard, flan (m) *flahn*
customer, cliente *klee-ehn'-teh*
customs, aduana *ah-doo-ah'-nah*
cut [wound], cuchillado *koo-chee-lyah'-doh*
cut v., cortar *kohr-tahr'*
cutlet, chuleta *choo-leh'-tah*

daily adj., cotidiano, diario *koh-tee-dyah'-noh,* *dee-ah'-ree-oh*
daily adv., diariamente *dee-ah-ryah-mehn'-teh*
damage v., hacer daño *ah-sehr' dah'-nyoh*
damaged, dañado *dah-nyah'-doh*
damp, húmedo *oo'-meh-doh* [8]
dance n., baile (m) *bah'-ee-leh*
dance v., bailar *bah-ee-lahr'*
danger, peligro *peh-lee'-groh*
dangerous, peligroso *peh-lee-groh'-soh*
dare v., osar *oh-sahr'*
dark, oscuro *oh-skoo'-roh*
darkness, oscuridad *oh-skoo-ree-dahd'*
date [time], fecha *feh'-chah;* [appointment], cita *see'-tah*
daughter, hija *ee'-hah* [3]
day, día (m) *dee'-yah* **per day, a day,** por día *pohr dee'-yah*
dead, muerto *mwehr'-toh*
dear, querido *keh-ree'-doh*
December, diciembre *dee-syehm'-breh*
decide, decidir *deh-see-deer'*
deck, cubierta *koo-byehr'-tah* [90]
declare, declarar *deh-klah-rahr'* [34]
deep, profundo *proh-foon'-doh*
deer, venado *veh-nah'-doh*
delay n., demora *deh-moh'-rah* [93]
delicious, delicioso *deh-lee-see-oh'-soh*

delighted, encantado *ehn-kahn-tah'-doh*
deliver, entregar *ehn-treh-gahr'*
dentist, dentista (m) *dehn-tees'-tah*
deodorant, desodorante (m) *dehs-oh-doh-rahn'-teh*
department store, almacenes *ahl-mah-seh'-nehs*
departure, salida *sah-lee'-dah* [88]
deposit *v.,* depositar *deh-spoh-see-tahr'* [45]
descend, bajar *bah-hahr'*
describe, describir *deh-skree-beer'*
desert *n.,* desierto *deh-syehr'-toh*
desire *v.,* desear *deh-seh-yahr'*
desk, escritorio *ehs-cree-toh'-ryoh*
dessert, postre (m) *pohs'-treh* [59]
destroy, destruir *dehs-troo-eer'*
detour, desvío *dehs-vee'-yoh*
develop, desarrollar *deh-sah-rroh-lyahr'*
dial *v.,* marcar *mahr-kahr'* [44, 45]
diamond, diamante (m) *dee-yah-mahn'-teh*
diaper, pañal (m) *pah-nyahl'*
diarrhea, diarrea *dee-yah-rreh'-yah*
dictionary, diccionario *deek-syoh-nah'-ryoh*
die *v.,* morir *moh-reer'*
difference, diferencia *dee-feh-rehn'-syah*
different, diferente *dee-feh-rehn'-teh*
difficult, difícil *dee-fee'-seel*
dine, comer *koh-mehr'* [56]
dining car, coche comedor (m) *koh'-cheh koh-meh-dohr'* [87]
dining room, comedor (m) *koh-meh-dohr'* [39, 90]
dinner, comida *koh-mee'-dah* [51, 52]
direct, directo *dee-rehk'-toh*
direction, dirección (f) *dee-rehk-syohn'*
director, director *dee-rehk-tohr'*
dirty, sucio *soo'-syoh* [57]
disappear, desaparecer *dehs-ah-pah-reh-sehr'*
discount *n.,* descuento *dehs-kwehn'-toh* [73]

discuss, discutir *dees-koo-teer'*
disease, enfermedad *ehn-fehr-meh-dahd'*
dish, plato *plah'-toh*
disinfect, desinfectar *dees-een-fehk-tahr'*
distance, distancia *dees-tahn'-syah*
district, barrio *bah'-rryoh*
disturb, molestar *moh-lehs-tahr'*
divorced, divorciado *dee-vohr-syah'-doh*
do, hacer *ah-sehr'* **how do you do?,** ¿cómo está usted?
    koh'-moh eh-stah' oo-stehd'?
dock, muelle (m) *mweh'-lyeh*
doctor, médico *meh'-dee-koh* [15, 94, 99]
dog, perro *peh'-rroh*
doll, muñeca *moo-nyeh'-kah*
dollar, dólar *doh'-lahr* [32]
done, hecho *eh'-choh*
donkey, burro *boo'-rroh*
door, puerta *pwehr'-tah* [87]
dose, dosis (f) *doh'-sees*
double, doble *doh'-bleh*
doubt, duda *doo'-dah* **no doubt,** sin duda *seen doo'-dah*
    without doubt, sin duda *seen doo'-dah*
down, abajo *ah-bah'-hoh* **to go down,** bajar *bah-hahr'*
downtown, centro ciudad *sehn'-troh syoo-dahd'* [48]
dozen, docena *doh-seh'-nah*
drawer, cajón (m) *kah-hohn'*
dress *n.,* vestido *vehs-tee'-doh* [71]
dress [oneself], vestirse *vehs-teer'-seh*
dressmaker, modista *moh-dees'-tah*
drink *n.,* bebida *beh-bee'-dah*
drink *v.,* beber *beh-behr'*
drive *v.,* manejar *mah-neh-hahr'* [47, 79]
driver, chofer *choh'-fehr* [46]
drop *v.,* dejar caer *deh-hahr' kah-ehr'*
druggist, farmacista *fahr-mah-sees'-tah*
drugstore, farmacia *fahr-mah'-syah* [95]

drunk, borracho *boh-rrah'-choh*

dry, seco *seh'-koh*

duck, pato *pah'-toh*

during, durante *doo-rahn'-teh*

dust, polvo *pohl'-voh*

duty, deber (m) *deh-behr'*; [tax], derechos de aduana *deh-reh'-chohs deh ah-doo-ah'-nah* [35]

dysentery, disentería *dee-sehn-teh-ree'-yah*

each, cada *kah'-dah*

each one, cada uno *kah'-dah oo'-noh*

eager, celoso *seh-loh'-soh*

ear, oreja, oído *oh-reh'-hah, oh-ee'-doh*

earache, dolor de oído *doh-lohr' deh oh-ee'-doh*

early, temprano *tehm-prah'-noh* [25]

earn, ganar *gah-nahr'*

earring, arete (m) *ah-reh'-teh*

earth, tierra *tyeh'-rrah*

easily, fácilmente *fah'-seel-mehn-teh*

east, este (m) *ehs'-teh*

Easter, pascua florida *pahs'-kwah floh-reε'-dah*

easy, fácil *fah'-seel*

eat, comer *koh-mehr'* [39, 51, 59]

edge, borde (m) *bohr'-deh*

egg, huevo *weh'-voh*

eight, ocho *oh'-choh*

eighteen, dieciocho *dyehs-ee-oh'-choh*

eighth, octavo *ohk-tah'-voh*

eighty, ochenta *oh-chehn'-tah*

either, qualquiera *kwahl-kyeh'-rah*   **either . . . or,** o . . . o . . . *oh . . . oh . . .*

elbow, codo *koh'-doh*

electric, eléctrico *eh-lehk'-tree-koh*

elevator, ascensor (m) *ah-sehn-sohr'* [40]

eleven, once *ohn'-seh*

else: nobody else, ningún otro *neen-goon' oh'-troh* **something else,** otra cosa *oh'-trah koh'-sah* **nothing else,** nada más *nah'-day mahs*
elsewhere, en otra parte *ehn oh'-trah pahr'-teh*
embark, embarcar *ehm-bahr-kahr'*
embarrassed, apenado *ah-peh-nah'-doh*
embassy, embajada *ehm-bah-hah'-dah*
embrace *v.,* abrazar *ah-brah-sahr'*
emergency, emergencia *eh-mehr-hehn'-syah*
empty, vacío *vah-see'-yoh*
end *n.,* fin (m) *feen*
engaged [busy], ocupado *oh-koo-pah'-doh*
engine, máquina *mah'-kee-nah*
English, inglés, inglesa *een-glehs', een-gleh'-sah* [10]
enjoy, gozar *goh-sahr'*
enormous, enorme *eh-nohr'-meh*
enough, bastante *bah-stahn'-teh* **that's enough,** basta *bah'-stah*
enter, entrar *ehn-trahr'*
entertaining, divertido *dee-vehr-tee'-doh*
entire, entero *ehn-teh'-roh*
entrance, entrada *ehn-trah'-dah*
envelope, sobre (m) *soh'-breh*
equal, igual *ee-gwahl'*
equipment, equipo *eh-kee'-poh*
error, error (m) *eh-rrohr'*
Europe, Europa *eh-oo-roh'-pah*
even *adv.,* aún *ah-oon'*
even [number], par *pahr*
evening, noche (f) *noh'-cheh* [102] **good evening,** buenas noches *bweh'-nahs noh'-chehs*
ever, alguna vez *ahl-goo'-nah vehs*
every, cada *kah'-dah* **every day,** cada día *kah'-dah dee'-yah* todos los días *toh'-dohs los dee'-yahs*
everyone, todo el mundo *toh'-doh ehl moon'-doh*
everything, todo *toh'-doh*

everywhere, en todas partes *ehn toh'-dahs pahr'-tehs*
evidently, evidentemente *eh-vee-dehn-teh-mehn'-teh*
exact, exacto *ehk-sahk'-toh*
examination, examen (m) *ehk-sah'-mehn*
examine, examinar *ehk-sah-mee-nahr'*
example, ejemplo *eh-hehm'-ploh*   **for example,** por ejemplo *pohr eh-hehm'-ploh*
excellent, excelente *ehk-seh-lehn'-teh*
except, excepto *ehk-sehp'-toh*
exchange *v.,* cambiar *kahm-byahr'*
exchange rate, cambio *kahm'-byoh* [32]
excursion, excursión (f) *ehs-koor-syohn'*
excuse *v.,* dispensar *dees-pehn-sahr'*   **excuse me,** dispénseme *dees-pehn'-seh-meh*
exercise, ejercicio *eh-hehr-see'-syoh*
exhibition, exposición (f) *ehs-poh-see-syohn'* [101]
exit, salida *sah-lee'-dah*
expect, esperar *ehs-peh-rahr'* [33]
expensive, caro, costoso *kah'-roh, kohs-toh'-soh* [39, 70]
explain, explicar *ehs-plee-kahr'*
explanation, explicación *ehs-plee-kah-syohn'*
export *v.,* exportar *ehs-pohr-tahr'*
express *adj.,* expreso *ehs-preh'-soh* [88]
extra, extra *ehks'-trah*
extraordinary, extraordinario *ehs-trah-ohr-dee-nah'-ryoh*
eye, ojo *oh'-hoh*

face, cara *kah'-rah*
factory, fábrica *fah'-bree-kah*
faint *v.,* desmayarse *dehs-mah-yahr'-seh*
fair [market], feria *feh'-ryah*
fall [season], otoño *oh-toh'-nyoh*
fall *n.,* caída *kah-ee'-dah*
fall *v.,* caer *kah-ehr'*
false, falso *fahl'-soh*
family, familia *fah-mee'-lyah*

famous, famoso, celibrado *fah-moh'-soh, seh-lee-brah'-doh*

fan, abanico *ah-bah-nee'-koh*

far, lejos *leh'-hohs* **so far,** hasta ahí *ah'-stah ah-ee'* **how far is it?,** ¿cuánto hay de aquí? *kwahn'-toh ah'-ee deh ah-kee'*

fare [cost], precio, tarifa *preh'-syoh, tah-ree'-fah* [48]

farewell, adiós *ah-dee-yohs'*

farm, granja, hacienda *grahn'-hah, ah-syehn'-dah*

farmer, granjero, agricultor *grahn-heh'-roh, ah-gree-koo-tohr'*

farther, más lejos *mahs leh'-hohs*

fashion, moda *moh'-dah*

fast [quick], rápido *rah'-pee-doh*

fasten, fijar *fee-hahr'* [92]

fat, gordo *gohr'-doh*

father, padre *pah'-dreh* [3]

father-in-law, suegro *sweh'-groh*

fault, culpa *kool'-pah*

favor, favor (m) *fah-vohr'*

favorite *adj. & n.,* favorito *fah-voh-ree'-toh*

fear: I fear, tengo miedo *tehn'-goh mee-eh'-doh*

feather, pluma *ploo'-mah*

February, febrero *feh-breh'-roh*

fee, honorarios (pl) *oh-noh-rah'-ryohs*

feel, sentir *sehn-teer'* [95]

feeling, sentimiento *sehn-tee-myehn'-toh*

female, hembra *ehm'-brah*

fence, cerca *sehr'-kah*

fender, guardafango *gwahr-dah-fahn'-goh*

ferry [boat], barco de trasbordo *bahr'-koh deh trahs-bohr'-doh*

fever, fiebre (m) *fyeh'-breh* [95]

few, pocos *poh'-kohs*

field, campo *kahm'-poh*

fifteen, quince *keen'-seh*

fifth, quinto *keen'-toh*

fifty, cincuenta *seen-kwehn'-tah*

fight *n.,* pelea *peh-leh'-yah*

fight *v.,* pelear *peh-leh-yahr'*

fill *v.,* llenar *lyeh-nahr'* [40]

filling [for a tooth], empaste (m) *ehm-pahs'-teh*

film, película *peh-lee'-koo-lah*

final, final *fee-nahl'*

finally, finalmente *fee-nahl-mehn'-teh*

find, encontrar, hallar *ehn-kohn-trahr', ah-lyahr'*

fine *adj.,* fino *fee'-noh*

fine *n.,* multa *mool'-tah* [79]

finger, dedo *deh'-doh* [95]

finish *v.,* acabar *ah-kah-bahr'*

fire, fuego *fweh'-goh*

first, primero *pree-meh'-roh* **first class,** primera clase *pree-meh'-rah klah'-seh* [86]

fish [in water], pez (m) *pehs;* [food], pescado *pehs-kah'-doh* [59]

fish *v.,* pescar *pehs-kahr'*

fish-bone, espina de pescado *ehs-pee'-nah deh pehs-kah'-doh*

fit [seizure], paroxismo *pah-rohk-sees'-moh*

fit *v.,* ajustar *ah-hoos-tahr'*

fitting [of a garment], prueba *proo-eh'-bah*

five, cinco *seen'-koh*

fix *v.,* arreglar *ah-rreh-glahr'* [77, 79]

flag, bandera *bahn-deh'-rah*

flashbulb, bombilla de cámara *bohm-bee'-lyah deh kah'-mah-rah*

flat, llano *lyah-noh*

flat tire, llanta desinflada *lyahn'-tah dehs-een-flah'-dah* [77]

flavor, sabor (m) *sah-bohr'*

flight, vuelo *vweh'-loh* [91, 92]

flint, pedernal *peh-dehr-nahl'*

flirt *v.*, coquetear *koh-keh-teh-yahr'*
flood, inundación *ee-noon-dah-syohn'*
floor, suelo *sweh'-loh;* [storey], piso *pee'-soh*
florist, florero, florista *floh-reh'-roh, floh-rees'-tah*
flower, flor (f) *flohr*
fluid, líquido, flúido *lee'-kee-doh, floo'-ee-doh*
fly [insect], mosca (f) *mohs'-kah*
fly *v.*, volar *voh-lahr'* [92]
fog, niebla *nyeh'-blah* [6]
follow, seguir *seh-geer'*
food, comida *koh-mee'-dah*
foot, pie (m) *pyeh*
for, por, para *pohr, pah'-rah*
forbid, prohibir *proh-ee-beer'*
forbidden, prohibido *proh-ee-bee'-doh*
forehead, frente (f) *frehn'-teh*
foreign, extranjero *ehs-trahn-heh'-roh*
foreigner, extranjero *ehs-trahn-heh'-roh*
forest, selva *sehl'-vah*
forget, olvidar *ohl-vee-dahr'*
forgive, perdonar *pehr-doh-nahr'*
fork, tenedor (m) *teh-neh-dohr'* [57]
form, forma *fohr'-mah*
former, anterior *ahn-teh-ryohr'*
formerly, antiguamente *ahn-tee-gwah-mehn'-teh*
fort, fuerte (m) *fwehr'-teh*
fortunate, afortunado *ah-fohr-too-nah'-doh*
fortunately, afortunadamente *ah-fohr-too-nah-dah-mehn'-teh*
forty, cuarenta *kwah'-rehn-tah*
forward, adelante *ah-deh-lahn'-teh*
fountain, fuente (f) *fwehn'-teh*
four, cuatro *kwah'-troh*
fourteen, catorce *kah-tohr'-seh*
fourth, cuarto *kwahr'-toh*
fracture *n.*, fractura *frahk-too'-rah*

fragile, frágil *frah'-heel*

free, libre *lee'-breh* [46]

freedom, libertad (f) *lee-behr-tahd'*

freeze, helarse *eh-lahr'-seh*

frequently, frecuentemente *freh-kwehn-teh-mehn'-teh*

fresh, fresco *frehs'-koh* [55]

Friday, viernes *vyehr'-nehs*

fried, frito *free'-toh*

friend, amigo (m), amiga (f) *ah-mee'-goh* (m), *ah-mee'-gah* (f) [2]

friendly, amistoso *ah-mɛɛ-stoh'-soh*

from, de, desde *deh, dehs'-deh*

front, frente (m) *frehn'-teh* **in front of,** delante de, en frente de *deh-lahn-teh deh, ehn frehn'-teh deh*

frozen, helado *eh-lah'-doh*

fruit, fruta *froo'-tah* [54]

full, lleno *lyeh'-noh*

fun, diversión *dee-vehr-syohn'*

function, función *foon-syohn'*

funnel, embudo *ehm-boo'-doh*

funny, cómico *koh'-mee-koh*

fur, piel (f) *pyehl*

furnished, amueblado *ah-mweh-blah'-doh*

furniture, muebles (m, pl) *mweh'-blehs*

further, más lejos *mahs leh'-hohs*

future, futuro *foot-too'-roh*

gain *v.,* ganar *gah-nahr'*

gamble *v.,* jugar *hoo-gahr'*

game, juego *hweh'-goh*

gangplank, plancha *plahn'-chah* [91]

garage, garage (m) *gah-rah'-heh* [78]

garden, jardín (m) *hahr-deen'*

garlic, ajo *ah'-hoh*

gas, gas (m), gasolina *gahs, gah-soh-lee'-nah*

gasoline, gasolina *gah-soh-lee'-nah* [76, 77]

gas station, puesto de gasolina *pwehs'-toh deh gah-soh-lee'-nah* [76]

gate, puerta *pwehr'-tah* [92]

gather [collect], recoger *reh-koh-hehr'*

gay, alegre *ah-leh'-greh*

general *adj.*, general *heh-neh-rahl'* **generally, in general,** en general *ehn heh-neh-rahl'*

generous, generoso *heh-neh-roh'-soh*

gentleman, caballero *kah-bah-lyeh'-roh*

get, conseguir *kohn-seh-geer'* **get in,** entrar *ehn-trahr'* **get off,** bajar *bah-hahr'* [48] **get on,** subir *soo-beer'* [48] **get up,** levantarse *leh-vahn-tahr'-seh* [98]

gift, regalo *reh-gah'-loh*

gin, ginebra *hee-neh'-brah*

girl, muchacha *moo-chah'-chah* [10]

give, dar *dahr* [13]

glad, contento *kohn-tehn'-toh*

gladly, con mucho gusto *kohn moo'-choh goo'-stoh*

glass [for drinking], vaso *vah'-soh* [54, 55, 58]

glasses [for the eyes], anteojos, gafas *ahn-teh-oh'-hohs, gah'-fahs*

glove, guante (m) *gwahn'-teh*

go, ir *eer* [12, 36, 47, 48, 89, 104] **go back,** volver *vohl-vehr'* **go in,** entrar *ehn-trahr'* **go out,** salir *sah-leer'*

God, Dios *dee-yohs'*

gold, oro *oh-roh*

good, bueno *bweh'-noh*

good-bye, adiós *ah-dee-yohs'*

government, gobierno *goh-byehr'-noh*

grandfather, abuelo *ah-bweh'-loh*

grandmother, abuela *ah-bweh'-lah*

grapes, uva, uvas *oo'-vah, oo'-vahs*

grapefruit, toronja *toh-rohn'-hah*

grass, hierba *yehr'-bah*

grateful, agradecido *ah-grah-deh-see'-doh*

gray, gris *grees* [70]

grease *n.*, grasa *grah'-sah*
great, grande *grahn'-deh*
green, verde *vehr'-deh* [70]
grocery, abacería *ah-bah-seh-ree'-yah*
ground, tierra *tyeh'-rrah*
group, grupo *groo'-poh*
grow, crecer *kreh-sehr'*
guard *v.*, guardar *gwahr-dahr'*
guest, invitado *een-vee-tah'-doh*
guide *n.*, guía (m) *gee'-yah* [101]
guilty, culpable *kool-pah'-bleh*
guitar, guitarra *gee-tah'-rrah*
gum [chewing], chicle (m), goma de masticar *cheek'-leh, goh'-mah deh mahs-tee-kahr'*
gun, fusil (m) *foo-seel'*

habit, costumbre (f) *kohs-toom'-breh*
hair, pelo, cabello *peh'-loh, kah-beh'-lyoh*
haircut, corte de pelo *kohr'-teh deh peh'-loh*
hairdresser, peinador (m) *peh-ee-nah-dohr'*
hairpin, horquilla *ohr-kee'-lyah*
half *n.*, mitad (f) *mee-tahd'*
half *adj.*, medio *meh'-dee-yoh*
hall, corredor (m) *koh-rreh-dohr'*
ham, jamón *hah-mohn'*
hand, mano (f) *mah'-noh*
handkerchief, pañuelo *pah-nyweh'-loh* [41]
hand-made, hecho a mano *eh'-choh ah-mah'-noh*
handsome, hermoso, guapo *ehr-moh'-soh, gwah'-poh* [10]
hang, hang up, colgar *kohl-gahr'*
hanger [for clothing], colgador de ropa *kohl-gah-dohr' deh roh'-pah*
happen, pasar *pah-sahr'* [16]
happy, feliz *feh-lees'*
harbor, puerto *pwehr'-toh* [89]
hard, duro *doo'-roh*

hardly [with difficulty], dificilmente *dee-fee-seel-mehn'-teh;* [not likely], improbablemente *eem-proh-bah-bleh-mehn'-teh*

harm *n.*, daño *dah'-nyoh*

harm *v.*, dañar *dah-nyahr'*

harmful, dañino *dah-nyee'-noh*

haste, prisa *pree'-sah*

hat, sombrero *sohm-breh'-roh*

hat shop, sombrerería *sohm-breh-reh-ree'-yah*

hate *v.*, odiar *oh-dee-yahr'*

have, tener *teh-nehr'* **I have,** tengo *tehn'-goh* **have you?** ¿tiene? *tyeh'-neh*

he, él *ehl*

head, cabeza *kah-beh'-sah*

headache, dolor de cabeza (m) *doh-lohr' deh kah-beh'-sah* [95]

health, salud (f) *sah-lood'* [58]

hear, oír *oh-eer'*

heart, corazón (m) *koh-rah-sohn'*

heat *n.*, calor (m) *kah-lohr'*

heavy, pesado *peh-sah'-doh*

heel, talón (m) *tah-lohn'*

hello, ¡hola! *oh'-lah*

help *n.*, ayuda *ah-yoo'-dah*

help *v.*, ayudar *ah-yoo-dahr'* [15]

helpful, útil *oo'-teel*

hem *n.*, dobladillo *doh-blah-dee'-lyoh*

hen, gallina *gah-lyee'-nah*

her, la, a ella *lah, ah eh'-lyah*

here, aquí *ah-kee'*

hers, suyo *soo'-yoh*

high, alto *ahl'-toh*

hill, colina, loma *koh-lee'-nah, loh'-mah*

him, le, lo, a él *leh, loh, ah ehl*

hip, cadera *kah-deh'-rah*

hire, alquilar *ahl-kee-lahr'* [75]

his, su, suyo *soo, soo'-yoh*
history, historia *ees-toh'-ree-yah*
hit *v.*, pegar *peh-gahr'*
hold, tener *teh-nehr'*
hole, agujero *ah-goo-heh'-roh*
holiday, día feriado *dee'-yah feh-ree-ah'-doh*
holy, santo *sahn'-toh*
home, hogar *oh-gahr'*
honest, honrado *ohn-rah'-doh*
honey [food], miel (f) *myehl*
honor, honor (m) *oh-nohr'*
hope *n.*, esperanza *ehs-peh-rahn'-sah*
hope *v.*, esperar *ehs-peh-rahr'* [3]
horn [automobile], bocina *boh-see'-nah*
hors d'oeuvres, entremeses (m, pl) *ehn-treh-meh'-sehs*
horse, caballo *kah-bah'-lyoh*
hospital, hospital (m) *ohs-pee-tahl'* [95]
host, anfitrión *ahn-fee-tree-yohn'*
hot, caliente *kah-lyehn'-teh*
hotel, hotel (m) *oh-tehl'* [10, 33, 37, 39, 47, 56, 73, 104]
hour, hora *oh'-rah*
house, casa *kah'-sah*
how, cómo *koh'-moh* **how are you?** ¿cómo está usted? *koh'-moh ehs-tah' oo-stehd'?* **how far?** ¿a qué distancia? *ah keh dees-tahn'-syah?* **how long?** ¿cuánto tiempo? *kwahn'-toh tyehm'-poh?* **how many?** ¿cuántos? *kwahn'-tohs?* **how much?** ¿cuánto? *kwahn'-toh?*
hug, *n.*, abrazo *ah-brah'-soh*
human, humano *oo-mah'-noh*
humid, húmedo *oo-meh-doh*
hundred, cien, ciento *syehn, syehn'-toh*
hunger, hambre (f) *ahm'-breh*
hungry: to be hungry, tener hambre *teh-nehr' ahm'-breh* [50, 51]
hurry *v.*, dar prisa *dahr pree'-sah* **hurry up,** de prisa *deh pree'-sah* [15]

hurt, doler *doh-lehr'* [95]
husband, esposo, marido *ehs-poh'-soh, mah-ree'-doh* [2]

I, yo *yoh*
ice, hielo *yeh'-loh* [58]
ice cream, helado *eh-lah'-doh* [59]
idea, idea *ee-deh'-yah*
identification, identificatión (f) *ee-dehn-tee-fee-kah-syohn'*
if, si *see*
ill, enfermo *ehn-fehr'-moh*
illegal, ilegal *ee-leh-gahl'*
illness, enfermedad *ehn-fehr-meh-dahd'*
imagine, imaginar *ee-mah-hee-nahr'*
immediately, inmediatamente *een-meh-dee-ah-tah-mehn'-teh*
important, importante *eem-pohr-tahn'-teh*
impossible, imposible *eem-poh-see'-bleh* [14]
improve, majorar *meh-hoh-rahr'*
improvement, mejoramiento *meh-hoh-rah-myehn'-toh*
in, en *ehn*
incident, incidente (m) *een-see-dehn'-teh*
included, incluído *een-kloo-ee'-doh* [59]
incomplete, incompleto *een-kohm-pleh'-toh*
inconvenient, inconveniente *een-kohn-veh-nyehn'-teh*
incorrect, erróneo *eh-rroh'-neh-oh*
increase *v.,* aumentar *ow-mehn-tahr'*
incredible, increíble *een-kreh-ee'-bleh*
indeed, de veras *deh veh'-rahs*
independence, independencia *een-deh-pehn-dehn'-syah*
independent, independiente *een-deh-pehn-dyehn'-teh*
indicate, indicar *een-dee-kahr'*
indigestion, indigestión (f) *een-dee-hehs-tyohn'*
indoors, en casa *ehn kah'-sah*
industrial, industrial *een-doos-tree-yahl'*
inexpensive, barato *bah-rah'-toh*
infection, infección *een-fehk-syohn'*

infectious, contagioso *kohn-tah-hyoh'-soh*
inform, informar *een-fohr-mahr'*
information, informes (m, pl) *een-fohr'-mehs*
injection, inyección (f) *een-yehk-syohn'*
injury, daño (m) *dah'-nyoh*
injustice, injusticia *een-hoos-tee'-syah*
ink, tinta *teen'-tah*
inn, fonda, posada *fohn'-dah, poh-sah'-dah*
inquire, preguntar *preh-goon-tahr'*
inside, dentro *dehn'-troh*
insist, insistir *een-sees-teer'*
inspect, revisar, inspeccionar *reh-vee-sahr', een-spehk-syoh-nahr'* [77]
instead of, en lugar de *ehn loo-gahr' deh*
institution, institución (f) *een-stee-too-syohn'*
insurance, seguro *seh-goo'-roh* [76]
insure, asegurar *ah-seh-goo-rahr'*
intelligent, inteligente *een-teh-lee-hehn'-teh*
intend, intentar *een-tehn-tahr'*
intense, intenso *een-tehn'-soh*
intention, intención (f) *een-tehn-syohn'*
interest *n.*, interés *een-teh-rehs'*
interest *v.*, interesar *een-teh-reh-sahr'*
interesting, interesante *een-teh-reh-sahn'-teh* [104]
intermission, entre acto *ehn'-treh ahk'-toh*
internal, interno *een-tehr'-noh*
international, internacional *een-tehr-nah-syoh-nahl'*
interpret, interpretar *een-tehr-preh-tahr'*
interpreter, intérprete *een-tehr'-preh-teh*
interview *n.*, entrevista *ehn-treh-vees'-tah*
into, en *ehn*
introduce, presentar *preh-sehn-tahr'*
introduction, introducción (f) *een-troh-dook-syohn'*
investigate, investigar *een-vehs-tee-gahr'*
invitation, invitación *een-vee-tah-syohn'*
invite, invitar *een-vee-tahr'*

iron [for ironing], plancha *plahn'-chah*
iron *v.*, planchar *plahn-chahr'*
iron [metal], hierro *yeh'-rroh*
is: he is, she is, it is, es, está *ehs, ehs-tah'*
island, isla *ees'-lah*
itch *v.*, picar *pee-kahr'*

jacket, chaqueta *chah-keh'-tah* [8]
jail, cárcel (f) *kahr'-sehl*
jam, marmelada *mahr-meh-lah'-dah*
January, enero *eh-neh'-roh*
jaw, quijada *kee-hah'-dah*
jelly, marmelada *mahr-meh-lah'-dah*
jewelry, joyas (f, pl) *hoh'-yahs*
jewelry store, joyería *hoh-yeh-ree'-yah*
job, empleo *ehm-pleh'-oh*
joke, broma *broh'-mah*
juice, jugo *hoo'-goh*
July, julio *hoo'-lyoh*
jump *v.*, saltar *sahl-tahr'*
June, junio *hoo'-nyoh*
just, justo *hoos'-toh*
justice, justicia *hoos-tee'-syah*

keep, guardar *gwahr-dahr'*
key, llave (f) *lyah'-veh* [35, 40, 76, 90]
kidneys, riñones (m) *ree-nyoh'-nehs*
kill, matar *mah-tahr'*
kilogram, kilogramo *kee-loh-grah'-moh*
kilometer, kilómetro *kee-loh'-meh-troh*
kind *adj.*, amable *ah-mah'-bleh*
kind *n.*, especie (f) *ehs-peh'-syeh*
king, rey *reh'-ee*
kiss *n.*, beso *beh'-soh*
kiss *v.*, besar *beh-sahr'*
kitchen, cocina *koh-see'-nah*

knee, rodillo *roh-dee'-lyoh*
knife, cuchillo *koo-chee'-lyoh* [57]
knock *v.,* llamar *lyah-mahr'*
know [something], saber *sah-behr';* [someone], conocer *koh-noh-sehr'* [10]

laborer, trabajador *trah-bah-hah-dohr'*
lace, encaje (m) *ehn-kah'-heh*
ladies' room, excusado para damas *ehs-koo-sah'-doh pah'-rah dah'-mahs*
lady, señora *seh-nyoh'-rah*
lake, lago *lah'-goh*
lamb, cordero *kohr-deh'-roh*
lame, cojo *koh'-hoh*
lamp, lámpara *lahm'-pah-rah*
land *n.,* tierra *tyeh'-rrah*
land *v.,* aterrizar *ah-teh-rree-sahr'* [93]
landing card, permiso de desembarque *pehr-mee'-soh deh dehs-ehm-bahr'-keh* [91]
language, idioma (m), lengua *ee-dee-yoh'-mah, lehn'-gwah*
large, grande *grahn'-deh*
last *adj.,* último *ool'-tee-moh*
last *v.,* durar *doo-rahr'* [101]
late, tarde *tahr'-deh* [25, 87]
laugh *n.,* risa *ree'-sah*
laugh *v.,* reír *reh-eer'*
laundry, lavandería *lah-vahn-deh-ree'-yah*
lavatory, excusado, retrete *ehs-koo-sah'-doh, reh-treh'-teh* [87]
law, ley (f) *leh'-ee*
lawyer, abogado *ah-boh-gah'-doh*
lazy, perezoso *peh-reh-soh'-soh*
lead *v.,* conducir *kohn-doo-seer'*
leaf, hoja *oh'-hah*
leak *n.,* escape (m) *ehs-kah'-peh*
learn, aprender *ah-prehn-dehr'*

least, mínimo *mee'-nee-moh*
leather, cuero *kweh'-roh*
leave [give up], dejar *deh-hahr'* [59, 76, 79]; [go away], salir
    sah-leer' [26, 41, 49, 86, 87, 88, 91]
left, izquierdo *ees-kyehr'-doh* [47]
leg, pierna *pyehr'-nah* [95]
lemon, limón (m) *lee-mohn'*
lend, prestar *prehs-tahr'*
length, largo *lahr'-goh*
lens, lente *lehn'-teh*
less, menos *meh'-nohs*
let, permitir *pehr-mee-teer'*
letter, carta *kahr'-tah* [42]
lettuce, lechuga *leh-choo'-gah*
liberty, libertad (f) *lee-behr-tahd'*
library, biblioteca *bee-blee-yoh-teh'-kah*
license, licencia *lee-sehn'-syah* [79]
lie: to lie down, acostarse *ah-kohs-tahr'-seh* [98]
lie [untruth], mentira *mehn-tee'-rah*
lie [tell an untruth], mentir *mehn-teer'*
life, vida *vee-dah*
lift *v.,* levantar *leh-vahn-tahr'*
light [weight], ligero *lee-heh'-roh;* [color], claro *klah'-roh*
light, luz (f) *loos*
lighter [for cigarettes], encendedor *ehn-sehn-deh-dohr'*
lightning, relámpago *reh-lahm'-pah-goh* [8]
like *adj.,* parecido *pah-reh-see'-doh*
like *v.,* gustar a *goos-tahr' ah* [7,37]   **I would like,** quisiera
    kee-syeh'-rah
line, línea *lee'-neh-yah* [45]
linen, lino *lee'-noh*
lip, labio *lah'-byoh*
lipstick, lápiz labial *lah'-pees lah-byahl'*
liqueur, licor *lee-kohr'*
list, lista *lees'-tah*
listen, eschuchar *ehs-koo-chahr'*

liter, litro *lee'-troh* [77]

little, pequeño *peh-keh'-nyoh* **a little,** un poco *oon poh'-koh* [11]

live *v.*, vivir *vee-veer'* [10, 103]

liver, hígado *ee'-gah-doh*

lobby, salón de entrada (m) *sah-lohn' deh ehn-trah'-dah*

lobster, langosta *lahn-goh'-stah*

long, largo *lahr'-goh* [71]

look *v.*, mirar *mee-rahr'*

loose, flojo *floh'-hoh* [72]

lose, perder *pehr-dehr'* [16, 42]

lost, perdido *pehr-dee'-doh*

lot: a lot of, mucho *moo'-choh* [102]

lotion, loción *loh-syohn'*

loud, ruidoso *roo-ee-doh'-soh*

love *n.*, amor (m) *ah-mohr'*

love *v.*, amar, querer *ah-mahr', keh-rehr'* [10]

low, bajo *bah'-hoh*

lubricate *v.*, lubricar *loo-bree-kahr'*

luck, suerte (f) *swehr'-teh* **good luck,** buena suerte *bweh'-nah swehr'-teh*

lucky, afortunado, feliz *ah-fohr-too-nah'-doh, feh-lees' to be lucky,** tener suerte *teh-nehr' swehr'-teh*

luggage, equipaje *eh-kee-pah'-heh* [36, 42, 46, 48]

lunch, almuerzo *ahl-mwehr'-soh* [51]

lung, pulmón (m) *pool-mohn'*

machine, máquina *mah'-kee-nah*

madam, señora *seh-nyoh'-rah*

magazine, revista *reh-vees'-tah*

mail *n.*, correo *koh-rreh'-oh* [33]

mailbox, buzón (m) *boo-sohn'*

main, principal *preen-see-pahl'* **main course,** plato principal *plah'-toh preen-see-pahl'*

major, mayor *mah-yohr'*

make, hacer *ah-sehr'*

male, masculino *mahs-koo-lee'-noh*
man, hombre *ohm'-breh* [10, 16]
manager, gerente *heh-rehn'-teh*
manicure, manicura *mah-nee-koo'-rah*
manner, manera *mah-neh'-rah*
manufactured, manufacturado *mah-noo-fahk-too-rah'-doh*
many, muchos *moo'-chohs*
map, mapa (m) *mah'-pah* [78]
marble, mármol (m) *mahr'-mohl*
March, marzo *mahr'-soh*
mark, marca *mahr'-kah*
market, mercado *mehr-kah'-doh*
marketplace, plaza de mercado *plah'-sah deh mehr-kah'-doh*
marmalade, marmelada *mahr-meh-lah'-dah*
married, casado *kah-sah'-doh*
marry, casarse con *kah-sahr'-seh kohn*
marvelous, maravilloso *mah-rah-vee-lyoh'-soh*
mass [church], misa *mee'-sah*
massage *n.,* masaje *mah-sah'-heh*
match, fósforo *fohs'-foh-roh* [72]
material, material (m) *mah-teh-ree-ahl'*
matter: no matter, no importe *noh eem-pohr'-teh* **what is the matter?** ¿qué hay? *keh ah'-ee*
May, mayo *mah'-yoh*
may, poder *poh-dehr'* **I may,** puedo *pweh'-doh* **may I?** ¿puedo? *pweh'-doh*
maybe, tal vez, quizás *tahl vehs, kee-sahs'*
me, me *meh* **to me,** me *meh* **with me,** conmigo *kohn-mee'-goh*
meal, comida *koh-mee'-dah* [39, 51, 56]
mean *v.,* significar *seeg-nee-fee-kahr'* [00]
measure *n.,* medida *meh-dee'-dah*
measure *v.,* medir *meh-deer'*
meat, carne (f) *kahr'-neh* [59]
mechanic, mecánico *meh-kah'-nee-koh* [77]

medicine, medicina *meh-dee-see'-nah* [99]
medium, medio *meh'-dee-yoh*
meet, encontrar *ehn-kohn-trahr'* [3]
melon, melón (m) *meh-lohn'*
member, miembro *myehm'-broh*
memory, memoria *meh-moh'-ree-yah*
mend, componer *kohm-poh-nehr'*
men's room, excusado para caballeros *ehs-koo-sah'-doh pah'-rah kah-bah-lyeh'-rohs*
mention *v.,* mencionar *mehn-syoh-nahr'*
menu, lista de platos *lees'-tah deh plah'-tohs* [52]
message, recado *reh-kah'-doh*
messenger, mensajero *mehn-sah-heh'-roh*
metal, metal (m) *meh-tahl'*
meter [measure], metro *meh'-troh*
middle, medio *meh'-dee-yoh*
midnight, medianoche *meh-dee-yah-noh'-cheh* [25]
mild, blando *blahn'-doh*
milk, leche (f) *leh'-cheh* [54, 55]
milliner, modista *moh-dees'-tah*
million, millón (m) *mee-lyohn'*
mind, mente (f) *mehn'-teh*
mine, mío *mee'-yoh*
mineral, mineral (m) *mee-neh-rahl'*
mineral water, agua mineral *ah'-gwah mee-neh-rahl'*
minute, minuto *mee-noo'-toh*
mirror, espejo *ehs-peh'-hoh* [76]
misfortune, desgracia *dehs-grah'-syah*
Miss, señorita *seh-nyoh-ree'-tah*
missing, perdido *pehr-dee'-doh*
mistake *n.,* error (m) *eh-rrohr'* [59]
mistaken, equivocado *eh-kee-voh-kah'-doh*
mix *v.,* mezclar *mehs-klahr'*
mixed, mezclado *mehs-klah'-doh*
model, modelo *moh-deh'-loh*
modern, moderno *moh-dehr'-noh*

modest, modesto *moh-dehs'-toh*

moment, momento *moh-mehn'-toh*

Monday, lunes (m) *loo'-nehs*

money, dinero *dee-neh'-roh* [16, 32, 33]

money order, giro postal *hee-roh pohs-tahl'*

monk, monje (m) *mohn'-heh*

month, mes (m) *mehs* **per month, a month,** por mes *pohr mehs*

monument, monumento *moh-noo-mehn'-toh* [103]

moon, luna *loo'-nah* [7]

more, más *mahs*

morning, mañana *mah-nyah'-nah* [102] **good morning,** buenos días *bwehn'-nohs dee'-yahs*

mosquito, mosquito *mohs-kee'-toh*

mosquito net, mosquitero *mohs-kee-teh'-roh*

most, el más, la más *ehl mahs, lah mahs* **most of,** la mayor parte de *lah mah-yohr' pahr'-teh deh*

mother, madre *mah'-dreh* [3]

motion, moción (f) *moh-syohn'*

motor, motor (m) *moh-tohr'*

mountain, montaña *mohn-tah'-nyah*

mouth, boca *boh'-kah*

move *v.*, mover *moh-vehr'* [17]

movie, cine (m) *see'-neh* [103]

Mr., señor *seh-nyohr'*

Mrs., señora *seh-nyoh'-rah*

much, mucho *moo'-choh* **very much,** muchísimo *moo-chee'-see-moh* **too much,** demasiado *deh-mah-syah'-doh* **how much?** ¿cuánto? *kwahn'-toh*

mud, fango *fahn'-goh*

muffler, silenciador *see-lehn-syah-dohr'*

muscle, músculo *moos'-koo-loh*

museum, museo *moo-seh'-oh* [48, 101]

mushroom, hongo *ohn'-goh*

music, música *moo'-see-kah*

musician, músico *moo'-see-koh*

must, deber, tener que *deh-behr', teh-nehr' keh*   **I must**
   debo, tengo que *deh'-boh, tehn'-goh keh*
mustache, bigote (m) *bee-goh'-teh*
mustard, mostaza *mohs-tah'-sah* [54]
mutton, carne de cordero *kahr'-neh deh kohr-deh'-roh*
my, mi *mee*
myself, yo mismo *yoh mees'-moh*

nail [fingernail], uña *oo'-nyah*
nailfile, lima *lee'-mah*
naked, desnudo *dehs-noo'-doh*
name, nombre (m) *nohm'-breh* [9]   **last name,** apellido
   ah-peh-lyee'-doh   **what is your name?** ¿cómo se llama?
   koh'-moh seh lyah'-mah   **my name is . . . ,** me llamo
   meh lyah'-moh
napkin, servilleta *sehr-vee-lyeh'-tah* [57]
narrow, estrecho *ehs-treh'-choh* [71, 72]
nation, nación (f) *nah-syohn'*
national, nacional *nah-syoh-nahl'*
nationality, nacionalidad *nah-syoh-nah-lee-dahd'*
native, nativo *nah-tee'-voh*
natural, natural *nah-too-rahl'*
naturally, naturalmente *nah-too-rahl-mehn'-teh*
nature, naturaleza *nah-too-rah-leh'-sah*
near, cerca *sehr'-kah*
nearly, casi *kah'-see*
necessary, necesario *neh-seh-sah'-ree-yoh*
neck, cuello *kweh'-lyoh*
necklace, collar (m) *koh-lyahr'*
necktie, corbata *kohr-bah'-tah*
need *v.,* necesitar *neh-seh-see-tahr'* [13] **I need,** necesito
   neh-seh-see'-toh
needle, aguja *ah-goo'-hah* [72]
neighbor, vecino *veh-see'-noh*
neighborhood, vecindario *veh-seen-dah'-ree-yoh*
neither . . . nor . . . , ni . . . ni . . . *nee . . . nee . . .*

nephew, sobrino *soh-bree'-noh*
nerve, nervio *nehr'-vee-yoh*
nervous, nervioso *nehr-vee-yoh'-soh*
never, nunca *noon'-kah*
nevertheless, sin embargo *seen ehm-bahr'-goh*
new, nuevo *nweh'-voh*
news, noticias (f, pl) *noh-tee'-syahs*
newspaper, periódico *peh-ree-yoh'-dee-koh*
next *adj.,* próximo *prohk'-see-moh*
next *adv.,* luego, después *lweh'-goh, dehs-pwehs'*
nice, simpático *seem-pah'-tee-koh*
niece, sobrina *soh-bree'-nah* [87]
night, noche (f) *noh'-cheh*   **good night,** buenas noches *bweh'-nahs noh'-chehs*
nightclub, café cantante *kah-feh' kahn-tahn'-teh*
nightgown, traje de dormir (m) *trah'-heh deh dohr-meer'*
nine, nueve *nweh'-veh*
nineteen, diecinueve *dyehs-ee-nweh'-veh*
ninety, noventa *noh-vehn'-tah*
ninth, nono *noh'-noh*
no, no *noh*
noise, ruido *roo-ee'-doh*
noisy, ruidoso *roo-ee-doh'-soh*
none [of persons], nadie *nah'-dee-yeh;* [of things], nada *nah'-dah*
noon, mediodía (m) *meh-dee-yoh-dee'-yah* [25]
no one, nadie *nah'-dee-yeh*
north, norte (m) *nohr'-teh*
northeast, nordeste (m) *nohr-dehs'-teh*
northwest, noroeste (m) *nohr-oh-ehs'-teh*
nose, nariz (f) *nah-rees'*
not, no *noh*
notebook, cuaderno *kwah-dehr'-noh*
nothing, nada *nah'-dah*   **nothing else,** nada más *nah'-dah mahs*
notice *n.,* aviso *ah-vee'-soh*

notice *v.*, notar *noh-tahr'*
notify, notificar *noh-tee-fee-kahr'*
novel [book], novela *noh-veh'-lah*
November, noviembre *noh-vyehm'-breh*
novocaine, novocaína *noh-voh-kah-ee'-nah*
now, ahora *ah-oh'-rah*
nowhere, en ninguna parte *ehn neen-goo'-nah pahr'-teh*
number, número *noo-meh'-roh* [40, 44]
nun, monja *mohn'-hah*
nurse, enfermera *ehn-fehr-meh'-rah*
nursemaid, niñera *nee-nyeh'-rah*
nut, nuez (f) *nwehs*

obey, obedecer *oh-beh-deh-sehr'*
obliged, obligado *oh-blee-gah'-doh*
obtain, obtenir *ohb-teh-neer'*
obvious, obvio *ohb'-vyoh*
occasionally, de vez en cuando *deh vehs ehn kwahn'-doh*
occupation, ocupación *oh-koo-pah-syohn'*
occupied, ocupado *oh-koo-pah'-doh* [87]
ocean, océano *oh-seh'-yah-noh* [39]
October, octubre *ohk-too'-breh*
odd [number], impar *eem-pahr'*; [unusual], raro *rah'-roh*
of, de *deh*
offer *v.*, ofrecer *ohf-reh-sehr'*
office, oficina *oh-fee-see'-nah*
official *adj.*, oficial *oh-fee-syahl'*
often, a menudo *ah meh-noo'-doh*
oil, aceite (m) *ah-seh'-ee-teh* [77]
old, viejo *vyeh'-hoh*
olive, aceituna *ah-seh-ee-too'-nah*
omelette, tortilla *tohr-tee'-lyah*
on, en *ehn*
once, una vez *oo'-nah vehs*
one, uno *oo'-noh*

one way [street], vía unica, tránsito *vee'-yah oo'-nee-kah, trahn'-see-toh*; [ticket], sólo ida *soh'-loh ee'-dah* [86]

onion, cebolla *seh-boh'-lyah*

only, sólo, solamente *soh'-loh, soh-lah-mehn'-teh*

open *adj.,* abierto *ah-byehr'-toh* [101]

open *v.,* abrir *ah-breer'* [35, 41, 64, 87, 102]

opera, ópera *oh'-peh-rah*

operation, operación (f) *oh-peh-rah-syohn'*

operator [telephone], telefonista *teh-leh-foh-nees'-tah*

opinion, opinión (f) *oh-pee-nyohn'*

opportunity, oportunidad (f) *oh-pohr-too-nee-dahd'*

opposite, opuesto *oh-pwehs'-toh*

optician, óptico *ohp'-tee-koh*

or, o, u *oh, oo*

orange, naranja *nah-rahn'-hah*

order *v.,* mandar *mahn-dahr'* **in order to,** para (plus infinitive) *pah'-rah*

ordinary, ordinario *ohr-dee-nah'-ryoh*

oriental, oriental *oh-ryehn-tahl'*

original, original *oh-ree-hee-nahl'*

ornament, ornamento *ohr-nah-mehn'-toh*

other, otro *oh'-troh*

ought, deber *deh-behr'*

our, ours, nuestro *nwehs'-troh*

out *adv.,* fuera *fweh'-rah* **to go out,** salir *sah-leer'*

outdoor, al aire libre *ahl ah'-ee-reh lee'-breh*

out of order, descompuesto *dehs-kohm-pwehs'-toh*

outside *adv.,* fuera, afuera *fweh'-rah, ah-fweh'-rah* **outside of,** fuera de *fweh'-rah deh*

over [ended] *adj.,* terminado *tehr-mee-nah'-doh*

over [above] *prep.,* sobre *soh'-breh*

overcharge *n.,* cargo excesivo *kahr'-goh ehk-seh-see'-voh*

overcoat, abrigo *ah-bree'-goh*

overcooked, cocinado en exceso *koh-see-nah'-doh ehn ehk-seh'-soh*

overhead, arriba *ah-rree'-bah*
overturn, volcar *vohl-kahr'*
owe, deber *deh-behr'* [59]
own *adj.,* propio *pro-pee'-yoh*
owner, dueño *dweh'-nyoh*
oyster, ostra *ohs'-trah*

pack *v.,* empaquetar *ehm-pah-keh-tahr'* [73]
package, paquete (m) *pah-keh'-teh*
page, página *pah'-hee-nah*
paid, pagado *pah-gah'-doh*
pain, dolor (m) *doh-lohr'*
paint, pintura *peen-too'-rah*
paint *v.,* pintar *peen-tahr'*
painting, pintura *peen-too'-rah*
pair, par, pareja *pahr, pah-reh'-hah* [72]
palace, palacio *pah-lah'-syoh* [103]
pale, pálido *pah'-lee-doh*
palm, palma *pahl'-mah*
pants, pantalones *pahn-tah-loh'-nehs*
paper, papel *pah-pehl'*
parcel, paquete (m) *pah-keh'-teh*
pardon, perdón (m) *pehr-dohn'* **pardon me,** dispénseme *dees-pehn'-seh-meh*
parents, padres (m, pl) *pah'-drehs*
park *n.,* parque (m) *pahr'-keh* [103]
park [a car] *v.,* estacionar *ehs-tah-syoh-nahr'* [79]
parsley, perejil (m) *peh-reh-heel'*
part, parte (f), pieza *pahr'-teh, pyeh'-sah*
part [leave] *v.,* partir *pahr-teer'*
particular, particular *pahr-tee-koo-lahr'*
partner [business], socio *soh'-syoh*
party, fiesta *fyehs'-tah*
pass *v.,* pasar *pah-sahr'*
passage, pasaje (m) *pah-sah'-heh*
passenger, pasajero *pah-sah-heh'-roh*

passport, pasaporte (m) *pah-sah-pohr'-teh* [16, 32, 34]

past *adj. & n.,* pasado *pah-sah'-doh*

pastry, pastelería *pahs-teh-leh-ree'-yah*

path, senda *sehn'-dah*

patient *adj. & n.,* paciente *pah-syehn'-teh*

pay *v.,* pagar *pah-gahr'* [35, 36, 59, 79] **pay cash,** pagar al contado *pah-gahr' ahl kohn-tah'-doh*

payment, pago *pah'-goh*

peace, paz (f) *pahs*

peaceful, pacífico *pah-see'-fee-koh*

peach, durasno, melocotón (m) *doo-rahs'-noh, meh-loh-koh-tohn'*

peak, cumbre (f) *koom'-breh*

peanut, cacahuete (m) *kah-kah-weh'-teh*

pear, pera *peh'-rah*

pearl, perla *pehr'-lah*

peasant, campesino *kahm-peh-see'-noh*

peas, guisantes (m) *gee-sahn'-tehs*

peculiar, peculiar *peh-koo-lyahr'*

pen, pluma *ploo'-mah* **fountain pen,** pluma fuente *ploo'-mah fwehn'-teh*

penalty, pena *peh'-nah*

pencil, lápiz (m) *lah'-pees*

penny, centavo *sehn-tah'-voh*

people, gente (f) *hehn'-teh*

pepper [spice], pimienta *pee-myehn'-tah*

peppermint, menta *mehn'-tah*

per, por *pohr*

perfect, perfecto *pehr-fehk'-toh*

performance, representación *reh-preh-sehn-tah-syohn'*

perfume, perfume *pehr-foo'-meh*

perfumery, perfumería *pehr-foo-meh-ree'-yah*

perhaps, quizá, quizás *kee-sah', kee-sahs'*

period, período *peh-ree'-yoh-doh*

permanent, permanente *pehr-mah-nehn'-teh*

permit *v.,* permitir *pehr-mee-teer'*

permission, permisión *pehr-mee-syohn'*
person, persona *pehr-soh'-nah*
personal, personal *pehr-soho-nahl'* [35]
perspiration, sudor (m) *so-dohr'*
petrol, gasolina *gah-soh-lee'-nah*
petticoat, enagua *eh-nah'-gwah*
pharmacist, farmacista (m) *fahr-mah-sees'-tah*
pharmacy, farmacia *fahr-mah'-syah*
photograph, fotografía *foh-toh-grah-fee'-yah*
photographer, fotógrafo *foh-toh'-grah-foh*
photography, fotografía *foh-toh-grah-fee'-yah*
photography shop, fotografería *foh-toh-grah-feh-ree'-yah*
piano, piano *pee-yah'-noh*
pick [choose], escoger *ehs-koh-hehr'*
pick up *v.,* recoger *reh-koh-hehr'*
picture, cuadro *kwah'-droh*
pie, pastel (m) *pah-stehl'*
piece, pedazo *peh-dah'-soh*
pier, muelle (m) *mweh'-lyeh* [89]
pig, puerco, cerdo *pwehr'-koh, sehr'-doh*
pigeon, paloma *pah-loh'-mah*
pile, montón (m) *mohn-tohn'*
pill, píldora *peel'-doh-rah*
pillar, pilar (m) *pee-lahr'*
pillow, almohada *ahl-moh-ah'-dah* [92]
pilot, piloto *pee-loh'-toh*
pin, alfiler (m) *ahl-fee-lehr* [72]   **safety pin,** imperdible
  eem-pehr-dee'-bleh
pineapple, piña *pee'-nyah*
pink, color de rosa *koh-lohr' deh roh'-sah*
pipe [tobacco], pipa *pee'-pah*
place *n.,* lugar (m) *loo-gahr'* [101]
place *v.,* poner *poh-nehr'*
plain [simple], sencillo *sehn-see'-lyoh*
plan *n.,* plan (m) *plahn*
plant, planta *plahn'-tah*

plastic, plástico *plah'-stee-koh*

plate, plato *plah'-toh*

platform, andén (m), plataforma *ahn-dehn', plah-tah-fohr'-mah* [86]

play *v.*, jugar *hoo-gahr'*

pleasant, agradable *ah-grah-dah'-bleh*

please: if you please, por favor, sírvase (plus the infinitive) *pohr fah-vohr', seer'-vah-seh* . . .

please [suit or satisfy], gustar, agradar *goos-tahr', ah-grah-dahr'* [3]

pleasure, placer (m), gusto *plah-sehr', goos'-toh* [4]

plenty of, mucho *moo'-choh*

plum, ciruela *see-rweh'-lah*

pneumonia, pulmonía *pool-moh-nee'-yah*

poached, escalfado *ehs-kahl-fah'-doh*

pocket, bolsillo *bohl-see'-lyoh*

pocketbook [wallet], cartera *kahr-teh'-rah;* [purse], bolsa *bohl'-sah*

point *n.*, punto *poon'-toh*

poison, veneno *veh-neh'-noh*

poisonous, venenoso *veh-neh-noh'-soh*

police, policía (f) *poh-lee-see'-yah* [16]

policeman, policía (m) *poh-lee-see'-yah*

police station, comisaría *koh-mee-sah-ree'-yah*

political, político *poh-lee'-tee-koh*

pond, laguna *lah-goo'-nah*

pool, piscina *pees-see'-nah*

poor, pobre *poh'-breh;* [inferior], malo *mah'-loh*

popular, popular *poh-poo-lahr'*

pork, puerco *pwehr'-koh*

port, puerto *pwehr'-toh* [89]

porter, mozo, portero *moh'-soh, pohr-teh'-roh* [36, 85 ,86]

portrait, retrato *reh-trah'-toh*

position, puesto *pwehs'-toh*

positive, positivo *poh-see-tee'-voh*

possible, posible *poh-see'-bleh* [14]

possibly, posiblemente *poh-see-bleh-mehn'-teh*
postage, franqueo *frahn-keh'-oh*
postage stamp, estampilla, sello *ehs-tahm-pee'-lyah, seh'-lyoh* [42]
postcard, tarjeta postal *tahr-heh'-tah pohs-tahl'*
post office, correo *koh-rreh'-oh*
potato, papa, patata *pah'-pah, pah-tah'-tah*
pound [money], libra *lee'-brah* [32]
powder, polvo *pohl'-voh* **face powder,** polvos *pohl'-vohs*
power, fuerza *fwehr'-sah*
powerful, fuerte *fwehr'-teh*
practical, práctico *prahk'-tee-koh*
practice n., práctica *prahk'-tee-kah*
prayer, oración (f) *oh-rah-syohn'*
precious, precioso *preh-syoh'-soh*
prefer, preferir *preh-feh-reer'* [70]
preferable, preferible *preh-feh-ree'-bleh*
pregnant, encinta *ehn-seen'-tah*
premier, primer ministro *pree-mehr' mee-nees'-troh*
preparation, preparación *preh-pah-rah-syohn'*
prepare, preparar *pre-pah-rahr'*
prepay, pagar adelantado *pah-gahr' ah-deh-lahn-tah'-doh*
prescription, receta *reh-seh'-tah* [99]
present [time], presente *preh-sehn'-teh*
present [gift], regalo *reh-gah'-loh*
present v., presentar *preh-sehn-tahr'* [2]
press [clothes] v., planchar *plahn-chahr'*
pressure, presión *preh-syohn'*
pretty, bonito *boh-nee'-toh* [10]
prevent, prevenir *preh-veh-neer'*
previous, previo *preh'-vyoh*
price, precio *preh'-syoh* [39]
priest, cura (m) *koo'-rah*
principal, principal *preen-see-pahl'*
prison, cárcel (f) *kahr'-sehl*
prisoner prisionero *pree-syoh-neh'-roh*

private, privado, confidencial *pree-vah'-doh, kohn-fee-dehn-syahl'*

prize, premio *preh'-myoh*

probable, probable *proh-bah'-bleh*

probably, probablemente *proh-bah-bleh-mehn'-teh*

problem, problema (m) *proh-bleh'-mah*

produce *v.*, producir *proh-doo-seer'*

production, producción (f) *proh-dook-syohn'*

profession, profesión (f) *proh-feh-syohn'*

professor, profesor *proh-feh-sohr'*

profit, beneficio *beh-neh-fee'-syoh*

program *n.*, programa (m) *proh-grah'-mah*

progress *n.*, progreso *proh-greh'-soh*

promenade, paseo *pah-seh'-oh*

promise *n.*, promesa *proh-meh'-sah*

prompt, pronto *prohn'-toh*

pronunciation, pronunciación (f) *proh-noon-syah-syohn'*

proof, prueba *prweh'-bah*

proper, propio *proh'-pee-yoh*

property, propiedad (f) *proh-pee-eh-dahd'*

proposal, propuesta *proh-pwehs'-tah*

proprietor, dueño *dweh'-nyoh*

prosperity, prosperidad (f) *prohs-peh-ree-dahd'*

protect, proteger *proh-teh-hehr'*

protection, protección (f) *proh-tehk-syohn'*

protestant, protestante *proh-tehs-tahn'-teh*

proud, orgulloso *ohr-goo-lyoh'-soh*

provide, proporcionar *proh-pohr-syoh-nahr'*

province, provincia *proh-veen'-syah*

provincial, provincial *proh-veen-syahl'*

provision, provisión *proh-vee-syohn'*

prune, ciruela pasa *see-rweh'-lah pah'-sah*

public, público *poo'-blee-koh*

publish, publicar *poo-blee-kahr'*

pull *v.*, tirar *tee-rahr'*

pump, bomba *bohm'-bah*

punish, castigar *kahs-tee-gahr'*
pupil, alumno, alumna *ah-loom'-noh, ah-loom'-nah*
purchase *n.,* compra *kohm'-prah*
purchase *v.,* comprar *kohm-prahr'*
pure, puro *poo'-roh*
purple, morado *moh-rah'-doh*
purpose *n.,* intención *een-tehn-syohn'*
purse, bolsa *bohl'-sah*
purser, comisario *koh-mee-sah'-ryoh*
push *n.,* empuje (m) *ehm-poo'-:|eh*
push *v.,* empujar *ehm-poo-hahr'*
put, poner *poh-nehr'* [77]

quality, calidad (f) *kah-lee-dahd'*
quantity, cantidad (f) *kahn-tee-dahd'*
quarrel *n.,* riña *reen'-yah*
quarrel *v.,* reñir *reh-nyeer'*
quarter *adj. & n.,* quarto *kwahr'-toh*
queen, reina *reh'-ee-nah*
question *n.,* pregunta *preh-goon'-tah*
quick, rápido *rah'-pee-doh*
quickly, de prisa, pronto *deh pree'-sah, prohn'-toh*
quiet, tranquilo *trahn-kee'-loh*
quite, bastante *bahs-tahn'-teh*

radio, radio (f) *rah'-dyoh*
railroad, ferrocarril (m) *feh-rroh-kah-rreel'*
railroad car, vagón (m) *vah-gohn'*
railroad station, estación de ferrocarriles *ehs-tah-syohn' deh feh-rroh-kah-rree'-lehs* [47, 85]
rain *n.,* lluvia, *lyoo'-vyah* [7]
rain *v.,* llover *lyoh-vehr'* **it's raining,** está lloviendo *eh-stah' lyoh-vyehn'-doh*
rainbow, arco iris *ahr'-koh ee'-rees* [7]
raincoat, impermeable (m) *eem-pehr-meh-ah'-bleh* [8]
raise *v.,* levantar *leh-vahn-tahr'*

ranch, hacienda, rancho *ah-syehn'-dah, rahn'-choh*
rapid, rápido *rah'-pee-doh*
rapidly, rápidamente *rah'-pee-dah-mehn-teh*
rare, raro *rah'-roh;* [undercooked], poco asado *poh'-koh ah-sah'-doh*
rash *n.,* erupción *eh-roop-syohn'*
raspberry, frambuesa *frahm-bweh'-sah*
rate, tarifa *tah-ree'-fah*
rather, más bien *mahs byehn*
raw, crudo *kroo'-doh*
razor, navaja de afeitar *nah-vah'-hah deh ah-feh-ee-tahr'*
razor blade, hojita de afeitar *oh-hee'-tah deh ah-feh-ee-tahr'*
reach *v.,* alcanzar *ahl-kahn-sahr'*
read, leer *leh-yehr'*
ready, listo, preparado *lees'-toh, preh-pah-rah'-doh* [52, 79]
real, verdadero *vehr-dah-deh'-roh*
really, verdaderamente *vehr-dah-deh-rah-mehn'-teh*
rear, de atrás *deh ah-trahs'*
reason *n.,* razón (f) *rah-sohn'*
reasonable, razonable *rah-soh-nah'-bleh*
receipt, recibo *reh-see'-boh* [33]
receive, recibir *reh-see-beer'*
recent, reciente *reh-syehn'-teh*
reception desk, recepción *reh-sehp-syohn'*
recognize, reconocer *reh-koh-noh-sehr'*
recommend, recomendar *reh-koh-mehn-dahr'* [52]
reconfirm [a flight], reconfirmar *reh-kohn-feer-mahr'* [92]
recover, recobrar *reh-koh-brahr'*
red, rojo *roh'-hoh* [70]
reduce, reducir *reh-doo-seer'*
reduction, rebaja *reh-bah'-hah*
refreshment, refresco *reh-frehs'-koh*
refund *v.,* reembolsar *reh-ehm-bohl-sahr'*
refuse *v.,* rehusar *reh-oo-sahr'*
region, región (f) *reh-hyohn'*

register n., registro *reh-hees'-troh*

register [a letter], certificar *sehr-tee-fee-kahr';* [at a hotel], registrarse *reh-hees-trahr'-seh*

regret v., lamentar *lah-mehn-tahr'*

regular, regular *reh-goo-lahr'*

regulation, reglamento *reh-glah-mehn'-toh*

relative [kin], pariente *pah-ree-yehn'-teh*

religion, religión (f) *reh-lee-hyohn'*

remark, observación (f) *ohb-sehr-vah-syohn'*

remember, recordar *reh-kohr-dahr'*

remove, quitar *kee-tahr'*

renew, renovar *reh-noh-vahr'*

rent v., alquilar *ahl-kee-lahr'*

repair v., reparar *reh-pah-rahr'*

repeat v., repetir *reh-peh-teer'* [11]

replace [put back], reponer *reh-poh-nehr';* [substitute], reemplazar *reh-ehm-plah-sahr'*

reply n., respuesta, contestación *rehs-pwehs'-tah, kohn-tehs-tah-syohn'*

republic, república *reh-poob'-lee-kah*

request v., pedir *peh-deer'*

rescue v., salvar *sahl-vahr'*

reservation, reservación *reh-sehr-vah-syohn'*

reserve v., reservar *reh-sehr-vahr'* [56]

reserved, reservado *reh-sehr-vah'-doh*

residence, residencia *reh-see-dehn'-syah*

resident, residente *reh-see-dehn'-teh*

responsible, responsable *reh-spohn-sah'-bleh*

rest n., descanso *dehs-kahn'-soh*

rest v., descansar *dehs-kahn-sahr'*

restaurant, restaurante (m) *rehs-tow-rahn'-teh* [39, 51]

restless, inquieto *een-kyeh'-toh*

rest room, excusado, retrete (m), *ehs-koo-sah'-doh, reh-treh'-teh*

result n., resultado *reh-sool-tah'-doh*

return, v., volver *vohl-vehr'*

return ticket, billete de ida y vuelta *bee-lyeh'-teh deh ee'-dah ee vwehl'-tah*

review n., revista *reh-vee'-stah*

reward, recompensa *reh-kohm-pehn'-sah*

rib, costilla *koh-stee'-lyah*

ribbon, cinta *seen'-tah*

rice, arroz (m) *ah-rrohs'*

rich, rico *ree'-koh*

ride n., paseo *pah-seh'-oh* [47]

right [correct], correcto *koh-rrehk'-toh* **to be right,** tener razón *teh-nehr' rah-sohn'* [12] **all right,** muy bien *mwee byehn*

right [direction], derecho *deh-reh'-choh* [47]

ring n., anillo, sortija *ah-nee'-lyoh, sohr-tee'-hah*

ring v., tocar, sonar *toh-kahr', soh-nahr'* [44]

ripe, maduro *mah-doo'-roh*

rise v., subir *soo-ber'*

river, río *ree'-yoh* [103, 104]

road, camino, carretera *kah-mee'-noh, kah-rreh-teh'-rah* [78]

roast [meat], asado *ah-sah'-doh*

rob, robar *roh-bahr'* [16]

robber, ladrón (m) *lah-drohn'*

rock, roca *roh'-kah* **on the rocks** (liquor), sobre hielo *soh'-breh yeh'-loh*

roll [bread], panecillo *pah-neh-see'-lyoh*

roll v., rodar *roh-dahr'*

roof, techo, tejado *teh'-choh, teh-hah'-doh*

room [of a house], cuarto *kwahr'-toh* [38]; [in a hotel], habitación *ah-bee-tah-syohn'* [38, 39, 40, 51]

rope, cuerda *kwehr'-dah*

rose, rosa *roh'-sah*

rouge, colorete (m) *koh-loh-reh'-teh*

rough, áspero *ahs'-peh-roh*

round, redondo *reh-dohn'-doh*

round trip, ida y vuelta *ee'-dah ee vwehl'-tah* [86]

royal, real *reh-yahl'*
rubber, caucho *kow'-choh*
rude, grosero *groh-seh'-roh*
rug, alfombra *ahl-fohm'-brah*
ruin *v.,* arruinar *ah-rroo-ee-nahr'*
rum, ron (m) *rohn*
run *v.,* correr *koh-rrehr'*
runway, pista *pee'-stah* [93]

sad, triste *tree'-steh*
safe, seguro *seh-goo'-roh*
safety pin, imperdible *eem-pehr-dee'-bleh*
sail *v.,* salir, zarpar *sah-leer', sahr-pahr'* [89]
sailor, marinero *mah-ree-neh'-roh*
saint, santo *sahn'-toh*
salad, ensalada *ehn-sah-lah'-dah*
sale, venta *vehn'-tah* [71] **for sale,** de venta *deh vehn'-tah*
salesgirl, vendedora *vehn-deh-doh'-rah*
salesman, vendedor *vehn-deh-dohr'*
salmon, salmón (m) *sahl-mohn'*
salt, sal (f) *sahl*
same, mismo *mees'-moh* **the same as,** lo mismo que *loh mees'-moh keh*
sample *n.,* muestra *mweh'-strah*
sand, arena *ah-reh'-nah*
sandwich, emparedado *ehm-pah-reh-dah'-doh*
sanitary, sanitario *sah-nee-tah'-ryoh*
sanitary napkin, toalla higiénica *toh-ah'-lyah ee-hyeh'-nee-kah*
satin, raso *rah'-soh*
satisfactory, satisfactorio *sah-tees-fahk-toh'-ryoh*
satisfied, contento, satisfecho *kohn-tehn'-toh, sah-tees-feh'-choh*
satisfy, satisfacer *sah-tees-fah-sehr'*
Saturday, sábado *sah'-bah-doh*

sauce, salsa *sahl'-sah*
saucer, platillo *plah-tee'-lyoh*
sausage, salchicha *sahl-chee'-chah*
save *v.,* ahorrar *ah-oh-rrahr';* [rescue], salvar *sahl-vahr'*
say, decir *deh-seer'* [11, 12]
scale, balanza *bah-lahn'-sah*
scar *n.,* cicatriz (f) *see-kah-trees'*
scarce, escaso *ehs-kah'-soh*
scarcely, apenas *ah-peh'-nahs*
scare *v.,* asustar *ah-soos-tahr'*
scarf, chalina *chah-lee'-nah*
scenery, paisaje (m) *pah-ee-sah'-heh*
scent *n.,* olor (m) *oh-lohr'*
schedule *n.,* horario *oh-rah'-ryoh*
school, escuela *ehs-kweh'-lah*
science, ciencia *syehn'-syah*
scientist, científico *syehn-tee'-fee-koh*
scissors, tijeras *tee-heh'-rahs*
scratch *n.,* rasguño *rahs-goo'-nyoh*
sculpture, escultura *eh-skool-too'-rah*
sea, mar (m) *mahr*
seafood, mariscos *mah-rees'-kohs*
seagull, gaviota *gah-vee-yoh'-tah*
seam, costura *koh-stoo'-rah*
seaport, puerto de mar *pwehr'-toh deh mar*
search *v.,* buscar *boos-kahr'*
seasick, mareado *mah-reh-ah'-doh* [91]
season, estación (f) *eh-stah-syohn'*
seat, asiento *ah-syehn'-toh* [87]
second, segundo *seh-goon'-doh* **second class,** segunda
  clase *seh-goon'-dah klah'-seh* [86]
secret *adj. & n.,* secreto *seh-kreh'-toh*
secretary, secretario *seh-kreh-tah'-ryoh*
section, sección *sehk-syohn'*
see, ver *vehr* [7, 101]
seem, parécer *pah-reh-sehr'*

select v., escoger, seleccionar *eh-skoh-hehr'*, *seh-lehk-syoh-nahr'*

selection, selección *seh-lehk-syohn'*

self, mismo *mees'-moh*

sell, vender *vehn-dehr'* [69, 72]

send, mandar, enviar *mahn-dahr'*, *ehn-vee-yahr'* [13, 73, 94]

sense v., sentir *sehn-teer'*

sensible, sensible *sehn-see'-bleh*

separate adj., separado *seh-pah-rah'-doh*

separate v., separar *seh-pah-rahr'*

September, septiembre *sehp-tyehm'-breh*

series, serie (f) *seh'-ree-yeh*

serious, serio *seh'-ryoh*

serve v., servir *sehr-veer'* [52, 66, 92]

service, servicio *sehr-vee'-syoh*   **service charge,** carga de servicio *kahr'-gah deh-sehr-vee'-syoh*

set [fixed], completado *kohm-pleh-tah'-doh*

set [place] v., arreglar, poner *ah-rreh-glahr'*, *poh-nehr'*

seven, siete *syeh'-teh*

seventeen, diecisiete *dyehs-ee-syeh'-teh*

seventh, séptimo *sehp'-tee-moh*

seventy, setenta *seh-tehn'-tah*

several, varios *vah'-ryohs*

severe, severo *seh-veh'-roh*

sew, coser *koh-sehr'*

shade, sombra *sohm'-brah*

shampoo, champú (m) *chahm-poo'*

shape n., forma *fohr'-mah*

share v., repartir *reh-pahr-teer'*

shark, tiburón (m) *tee-boo-rohn'*

sharp, agudo *ah-goo'-doh*

shave n., afeitada *ah-feh-ee-tah'-dah*

shave v., afeitar, afeitarse *ah-feh-ee-tahr'*, *ah-feh-ee-tahr'-seh*

shaving cream, crema de afeitar *kreh'-mah deh ah-feh-ee-tahr'*

she, ella *eh'-lyah*

sheep, carnero *kahr-neh'-roh*

sheet [of paper], hoja *oh'-hah;* [bed sheet], sábana *sah'-bah-nah*

shellfish, mariscos *mah-rees'-kohs*

shelter, refugio *reh-foo'-hyoh*

sherry, jérez *heh'-rehs*

shine *v.,* brillar *bree-lyahr'*

ship *n.,* buque, vapor *boo'-keh, vah-pohr'* [89, 91]

ship *v.,* enviar *ehn-vee-yahr'* [73]

shiver *v.,* tiritar *tee-ree-tahr'*

shirt, camisa *kah-mee'-sah* [41, 71]

shock *n.,* choque (m) *choh'-keh*

shoe, zapato *sah-pah'-toh* [71, 72]

shoelace, cordón (m) *kohr-dohn'*

shoeshine, lustre (m) *loos'-treh*

shoestore, zapatería *sah-pah-teh-ree'-yah*

shoot *v.,* tirar *tee-rahr'*

shop *n.,* tienda *tyehn'-dah*

shop: to go shopping, ir de compras *eer deh kohm'-prahs* [64]

shopping center, centro de compras *sehn'-troh deh kohm'-prahs* [104]

shore, orilla *oh-ree'-lyah*

short, corto *kohr'-toh* [71]

shorts, calzoncillos (m, pl) *kahl-sohn-see'-lyohs*

shoulder, hombro *ohm'-broh*

show *n.,* exhibición, espectáculo *ehk-see-bee-syohn', eh-spehk-tah'-koo-loh*

show *v.,* mostrar *moh-strahr'* [13, 69, 97]

shower [bath], ducha *doo'-chah* [38]

shrimp, camarón (m) *kah-mah-rohn'*

shut *adj.,* cerrado *seh-rrah'-doh*

shut *v.,* cerrar *seh-rrahr'*

shy, tímido *tee'-mee-doh*

sick, enfermo *ehn-fehr'-moh* [95]

side [of object], lado *lah'-doh;* [of person], costado *kohs-tah'-doh*

sidewalk, acera, banqueta *ah-seh'-rah, bahn-keh'-tah*

sight, vista *vee'-stah*

sightseeing, visita de puntos de interés *vee-see'-tah deh poon'-tohs deh een-teh-rehs'* [100]

sign *n.*, letrero *leh-treh'-roh*

sign *v.*, firmar *feer-mahr'* [33]

signature, firma *feer'-mah*

silence, silencio *see-lehn'-syoh*

silent, silencioso *see-lehn-syoh'-soh*

silk, seda *seh'-dah*

silly, tonto *tohn'-toh*

silver, plata *plah'-tah*

similar, semejante, parecido *seh-meh-hahn'-teh, pah-reh-see'-doh*

simple, sencillo *sehn-see'-lyoh*

since, desde *dehs'-deh*

sing, cantar *kahn-tahr'*

single, solo *soh'-loh*

sir, señor *seh-nyohr'*

sister, hermana *ehr-mah'-nah* [3]

sit, sentarse *sehn-tahr'-seh* [102]

situation, situación (f) *see-too-ah-syohn'*

six, seis *seh'-ees*

sixteen, dieciséis *dyehs'-ee-seh'-ees*

sixth, sexto *seh'-stoh*

sixty, sesenta *seh-sehn'-tah*

size, tamaño, medida *tah-mah'-nyoh, meh-dee'-dah* [69]

skilled, skillful, hábil *ah'-beel*

skin, piel (f) *pyehl*

skirt, falda *fahl'-dah* [71]

skull, cráneo *krah'-neh-oh*

sky, cielo *syeh'-loh*

sleep *n.*, sueño *sweh'-nyoh*

sleep *v.*, dormir *dohr-meer'* [99]

sleeve, manga *mahn'-gah* [71]
slice *n.,* tajada *tah-hah'-dah*
slice *v.,* tajar *tah-hahr'*
slight, ligero *lee-heh'-roh*
slip [garment], combinación *kohm-bee-nah-syohn'*
slip *v.,* resbalarse *rehs-bah-lahr'-seh*
slippers, zapatillas *sah-pah-tee'-lyahs*
slippery, resbaloso *rehs-bah-loh'-soh* [78]
slow, lento *lehn'-toh*
slowly, despacio *dehs-pah'-syoh* [11, 47]
small, pequeño *peh-keh'-nyoh*
smart, listo *lee'-stoh*
smell *n.,* olor (m) *oh-lohr'*
smell, *v.,* oler *oh-lehr'*
smile *n.,* sonrisa *sohn-ree'-sah*
smile *v.,* sonreir *sohn-reh-eer'*
smoke *n.,* humo *oo'-moh*
smoke *v.,* fumar *foo-mahr'* [92, 98, 99]
smooth, liso *lee'-soh*
snack, bocadillo *boh-kah-dee'-lyoh*
snow, nieve (f) *nyeh'-veh* **it's snowing,** está nevando *eh-stah' neh-vahn'-doh*
so, así, tan *ah-see', tahn* **so that,** así que *ah-see' keh* **so as,** para (plus infinitive) *pah'-rah*
soap, jabón (m) *hah-bohn'* [41]
social, social *soh-syahl'*
sock, calcetín (m) *kahl-seh-teen'*
soda, soda *soh'-dah*
soft, blando *blahn'-doh*
sold, vendido *vehn-dee'-doh*
solid, sólido *soh'-lee-doh*
some, algún *ahl-goon'*
somehow, de algún modo *deh ahl-goon' moh'-doh*
someone, alguien *ahl'-gyehn*
something, algo *ahl'-goh*
sometimes, algunas veces *ahl-goo'-nahs veh'-sehs*

somewhere, en alguna parte *ehn ahl-goo'-nah pahr'-teh*

son, hijo *ee'-hoh* [3]

song, canción (f) *kahn-syohn'*

soon, pronto *prohn'-toh*

sore, *adj.,* dolorido *doh-loh-ree'-doh*

sore throat, dolor de garganta (m) *doh-lohr' deh gahr-gahn'-tah*

sorrow, pena *peh'-nah*

sorry, apenado *ah-peh-nah'-doh* **to be sorry,** sentir *sehn-teer'* [3]

sort, clase (f) *klah'-seh*

soul, alma *ahl'-mah*

sound *n.,* sonido *soh-nee'-doh*

soup, sopa *soh'-pah* [57]

sour, agrio *ahg'-ryoh* [55]

south, sud (m) *sood*

southeast, sudeste *sood-eh'-steh*

southwest, sudoeste *sood-oh-eh'-steh*

souvenir, recuerdo *reh-kwehr'-doh*

Spanish, español *eh-spah-nyohl'*

speak, hablar *ahb-lahr'* **do you speak English?** ¿habla inglés? *ah'-blah een-glehs'*

special, especial *eh-speh-syahl'*

specialty, especialidad (f) *eh-speh-syah-lee-dahd'*

speed, velocidad (f) *veh-loh-see-dahd'* [78]

spell *v.,* deletrear *deh-leh-treh-ahr'*

spend, gastar *gahs-tahr'*

spicy, picante *pee-kahn'-teh*

spinach, espinaca *eh-spee-nah'-kah*

spine, espina *eh-spee'-nah*

splendid, espléndido *eh-splehn'-dee-doh*

spoiled, dañado *dah-nyah'-doh*

spoon, cuchara *koo-chah'-rah* [57]

spot *n.,* mancha *mahn'-chah*

sprain *n.,* torcedura *tohr-seh-doo'-rah*

spring [season], primavera *pree-mah-veh'-rah*

spring [for water], fuente (f) *fwehn'-teh*
springs [of a car], muelles (m, pl) *mweh'-lyehs*
square *adj.*, cuadrado *kwahd-rah'-doh*
square [public], plaza *plah'-sah* [102]
stairs, escalera *eh-skah-leh'-rah*
stamp, estampilla, sello *eh-stahm-pee'-lyah, seh'-lyoh* [42]
stand *v.*, estar de pie *eh-stahr' deh pyeh*
star, estrella *eh-streh'-lyah* [7]
starch, almidón (m) *ahl-mee-dohn'*
start *n.*, principio *preen-see'-pyoh*
start *v.*, empezar *ehm-peh-sahr'*
state, estado *eh-stah'-doh*
stateroom, camarote (m) *kah-mah-roh'-tèh* [90]
station, estación (f) *eh-stah-syohn'* [87]
statue, estatua *eh-stah'-too-wah*
stay *v.*, parar, quedarse *pah-rahr', keh-dahr'-seh* [17, 39, 40]; [lodge], hospedarse *ohs-peh-dahr'-seh* [10]
steak, biftec (m), filete (m) *beef'-tehk, fee-leh'-teh*
steal *v.*, robar *roh-bahr'* [16]
steel, acero *ah-seh'-roh*
steep, empinado *ehm-eep-nah'-doh*
step, paso *pah'-soh*
stew, guisado *gee-sah'-doh*
steward, camarero *kah-mah-reh'-roh* [90]
stick *n.*, palo *pah'-loh*
stiff, tieso *tyeh'-soh*
still [quiet], quieto *kyeh'-toh*
still [yet], todavía *toh-dah-vee'-yah*
sting *n.*, picadura *pee-kah-doo'-rah*
sting *v.*, picar *pee-kahr'*
stockings, medias *meh'-dee-yahs*
stolen, robado *roh-bah'-doh*
stomach, estómago *eh-stoh'-mah-goh* [95]
stone, piedra *pyeh'-drah*
stop *n.*, parada *pah-rah'-dah*
stop *v.*, parar *pah-rahr'* [15, 47, 48, 87]

store *n.*, tienda *tyehn'-dah* [64, 101]

storm, tempestad (f) *tehm-peh-stahd'*

story, historia *ee-stoh'-ryah*

straight, derecho *deh-reh'-choh* **straight ahead,** todo seguido *toh'-doh seh-gee'-doh* [48]

strange, estraño *eh-strah'-nyoh*

stranger, extranjero *eh-strahn-heh'-roh*

strawberry, fresa *freh'-sah*

stream, arroyo *ah-rroh'-yoh*

street, calle (f) *kah'-lyeh* [38, 48, 102, 103]

streetcar, tranvía (m) *trahn-vee'-yah*

strength, fuerza *fwehr'-sah*

string, cuerda *kwehr'-dah*

strong, fuerte *fwehr'-teh*

structure, estructura *ehs-trook-too'-rah*

student, estudiante *ehs-too-dee-yahn'-teh*

study *v.*, estudiar *eh-stoo-dee-yahr'*

style, estilo *eh-stee'-loh*

suburb, suburbio *soo-boor'-bee-yoh*

succeed [follow], suceder *soo-seh-dehr';* [attain one's goal], tener buen éxito *teh-nehr' bwehn ehk'-see-toh*

success, éxito *ehk'-see-toh*

such, tal *tahl*

suddenly, de repente *deh reh-pehn'-teh*

suffer, sufrir *soo-freer'*

sufficient, suficiente *soo-fee-syehn'-teh*

sugar, azúcar (m) *ah-soo'-kahr* [52, 54]

suggest, sugerir *soo-heh-reer'*

suggestion, sugestión (f) *soo-hehs-tyohn'*

suit, traje (m) *trah'-heh*

suitcase, maleta *mah-leh'-tah* [40]

summer, verano *veh-rah'-noh*

sun, sol (m) *sohl* [6]

sunburn, quemado por el sol *keh-mah'-doh pohr ehl sohl*

Sunday, domingo *doh-meen'-goh*

sunglasses, gafas contra el sol *gah'-fahs kohn'-trah ehl sohl*

sunny, asoleado *ah-soh-leh-ah'-doh*
supper, cena *seh'-nah* [51]
sure, seguro *seh-goo'-roh*
surface, superficie *soo-pehr-fee'-syeh*
surprise *n.,* sorpresa *sohr-preh'-sah*
surprise *v.,* sorprender *sohr-prehn-dehr'*
suspect *v.,* sospechar *soh-speh-chahr'*
suspicion, sospecha *sohs-peh'-chah*
sweater, suéter *sweh'-tehr* [8]
sweep, barrer *bah-rrehr'*
sweet, dulce *dool'-seh*
swim *v.,* nadar *nah-dahr'* [104]
swollen, hinchado *een-chah'-doh*

table, mesa *meh'-sah* [52, 56, 59, 90]
tablecloth, mantel (m) *mahn-tehl'* [59]
tailor, sastre (m) *sahs'-treh*
take, tomar *toh-mahr'* **take off,** quitarse *kee-tahr'-seh*
  [92]
talk, hablar *ahb-lahr'*
tall, alto *ahl'-toh*
tank, tanque (m) *tahn'-keh*
taste *n.,* gusto *goo'-stoh*
taste *v.,* gustar *goo-stahr'*
tax *n.,* impuesto *eem-pweh'-stoh*
taxi, taxi *tahk'-see* [46]
tea, té (m) *teh* [55]
teach *v.,* enseñar *ehn-seh-nyahr'*
teacher, maestro *mah-eh'-stroh*
tear [drop], lágrima *lah'-gree-mah*
tear *v.,* desgarrar *dehs-gah-rrahr'*
teaspoon, cucharita *koo-chah-ree'-tah*
teeth, dientes *dyehn'-tehs*
telegram, telegrama (m) *teh-leh-grah'-mah*
telephone, teléfono *teh-leh'-foh-noh* [43]

telephone booth, cabina telefónica *kah-bee'-nah teh-leh-foh'-nee-kah*

telephone operator, telefonista *teh-leh-foh-nee'-stah*

television, televisión *teh-leh-vee-syohn'*

tell *v.,* decir *deh-seer'* [13, 48]

temperature, temperatura *tehm-peh-rah-too'-rah*

temple, templo *tehm'-ploh*

temporary, temporario *tehm-poh-rah'-ryoh*

ten, diez *dyehs*

tendon, tendón (m) *tehn-dohn'*

tenth, décimo *deh'-see-moh*

test, prueba *prweh'-bah*

than, que *keh*

thank, agradecer *ah-grah-deh-sehr'* [104]

thank you, gracias *grah'-syahs*

thankful, agradecido *ah-grah-deh-see'-doh*

that *rel.,* que *keh*

that *pron.,* ese, esa *eh'-seh, eh'-sah*

the, el (m), la (f), los (m, pl), las (f, pl) *ehl, lah, lohs, lahs*

theater, teatro *teh-ah'-troh* [103]

theft, robo *roh'-boh*

their, su *soo*

theirs, suyo *soo'-yoh*

them [used of persons], los (m), las (f) *lohs, lahs*

then, entonces *ehn-tohn'-sehs*

there *adv.,* allá, allí *ah-lyah', ah-lyee'*   **there is, there are,** hay *ah'-ee*

therefore, por eso *pohr eh'-soh*

thermometer, termómetro *tehr-moh'-meh-troh*

these, estos, estas *eh'-stohs, eh'-stahs*

they, ellos, ellas *eh'-lyohs, eh'-lyahs*

thick, espeso *eh-speh'-soh*

thigh, muslo *moos'-loh*

thin, delgado, flaco *dehl-gah'-doh, flah'-koh*

thing, cosa *koh'-sah*

think, pensar *pehn-sahr'*

third, tercero *tehr-seh'-roh*

thirst, sed (f) *sehd*

thirsty: to be thirsty, tener sed *teh-nehr' sehd* [50, 51]

thirteen, trece *treh'-seh*

thirty, treinta *treh'-een-tah*

this, este, esta *eh'-steh, eh'-stah*

those, esos, esas *eh'-sohs, eh'-sahs*

thoroughfare, pasaje (m) *pah-sah'-heh*

thousand, mil *meel*

thread, hilo *ee'-loh* [72]

three, tres *trehs*

throat, garganta *gahr-gahn'-tah*

through *prep.,* a través de *ah trah-vehs' deh*

through [finished], terminado *tehr-mee-nah'-doh*

throw, tirar *tee-rahr'*

thumb, pulgar (m) *pool-gahr'*

thunder, trueno *trweh'-noh*

Thursday, jueves *hweh'-vehs*

ticket, billete (m) *bee-lyeh'-teh* [86, 88, 92]

ticket office, despacho de billetes *dehs-pah'-choh deh bee-lyeh'-tehs* [86]

tie [bind], liar *lee-ahr'*

tight, apretado *ah-preh-tah'-doh* [72]

tighten, apretar *ah-preh-tahr'*

till, hasta *ah'-stah*

time, tiempo *tyehm'-poh*   **what time is it?** ¿qué hora es? *keh oh'-rah ehs*   **on time,** a tiempo *ah tyehm'-poh*

timetable, horario *oh-rah'-ryoh* [86]

tip [money], propina *proh-pee'-nah* [59]

tire [of a car], llanta *lyahn'-tah*   **flat tire,** llanta desinflada *lyahn'-tah dehs-een-flah'-dah*

tire *v.,* cansar *kahn-sahr'*

tired, cansado *kahn-sah'-doh* [102]

to, a *ah*

toast, pan tostado *pahn toh-stah'-doh*

tobacco, tabaco *tah-bah'-koh* [35]

tobacconist, tabaquería *tah-bah-keh-ree'-yah*
today, hoy *oy* [101]
toe, dedo del pie *deh'-doh dehl pyeh*
together, juntos *hoon'-tohs*
toilet, excusado, retrete *ehs-koo-sãh'-doh, reh-treh'-teh*
toilet paper, papel higiénico *pah-pehl' ee-hyeh'-nee-koh*
tomato, tomate (m) *toh-mah'-teh*
tomorrow, mañana *mah-nyah'-nah* [3, 41, 99]
tongue, lengua *lehn'-gwah* [97]
tonight, esta noche *eh'-stah noh'-cheh*
tonsil, tonsila *tohn-see'-lah*
too [also], también *tahm-byehn'*
too [much], demasiado *deh-mah-syah'-doh*
tooth, diente (m) *dyehn'-teh*
toothache, dolor de dientes *doh-lohr' deh dyehn'-tehs*
toothbrush, cepillo de dientes *seh-pee'-lyoh deh dyehn'-tehs*
toothpaste, pasta dentífrica *pah'-stah dehn-tee'-free-kah*
top, pico *pee'-koh*
toreador, torero *toh-reh'-roh*
torn, roto *roh'-toh*
total, *adj. & n.,* total (m) *toh-tahl'*
touch *v.,* tocar *toh-kahr'*
tough, duro *doo'-roh*
tour, excursión (f) *ehk-skoor-syohn'* [101, 104]
tow *v.,* remolcar *reh-mohl-kahr'*
toward, hacia *ah'-syah*
towel, toalla *toh-ah'-lyah* [41]
town, pueblo *pweh'-bloh*
toy, juguete (m) *hoo-geh'-teh*
toy shop, tienda de juguetes *tyehn'-dah deh hoo-geh-tehs*
trade *n.,* comercio *koh-mehr'-syoh*
traffic, tráfico *trah'-fee-koh*
train *n.,* tren (m) *trehn* [16, 85–88]
transfer *v.,* transbordar *trahns-bohr-dahr'* [49]
translate *v.,* traducir *trah-doo-seer'*

translation, traducción (f) *trah-dook-syohn'*
translator, traductor (m) *trah-dook-tohr'*
transmission, transmisión *trahns-mee-syohn'*
transportation, transportación (f) *trahns-pohr-tah-syohn'*
travel *v.*, viajar *vyah-hahr'*
traveler, viajero *vyah-heh'-roh*
travelers' check, cheque de viajeros *cheh'-keh deh vyah-heh'-rohs* [32]
tray, bandeja *bahn-deh'-hah*
tree, árbol (m) *ahr'-bohl*
trip, viaje (m) *vyah'-heh* [91]
tropical, tropical *troh-pee-kahl'*
trousers, pantalones *pahn-tah-loh'-nehs*
truck, camión (m) *kah-myohn'*
true, verdadero *vehr-dah-deh'-roh*
trunk, baúl (m) *bah-ool'*
truth, verdad (f) *vehr-dahd'*
try *v.*, ensayar *ehn-sah-yahr'*   **try on,** probar *proh-bahr'* [69]
Tuesday, martes *mahr'-tehs*
turn *n.*, vuelta *vwehl'-tah*
turn *v.*, voltear *vohl-teh-ahr'* [47]
twelve, doce *doh'-seh*
twenty, veinte *veh'-een-teh*
twice, dos veces *dohs. veh'-sehs*
twin beds, camas gemelas *kah'-mahs heh-meh'-lahs*
two, dos *dohs*

ugly, feo *feh'-yoh*
umbrella, paraguas (m) *pah-rah'-gwahs* [8]
uncle, tío *tee'-yoh*
uncomfortable, incómodo *een-koh'-moh-doh*
unconscious, inconsciente *een-kohn-syehn'-teh*
under *prep.*, debajo de *deh-bah'-hoh deh*
underneath *prep.*, debajo *deh-bah'-hoh*
undershirt, camisola· *kah-mee-soh'-lah*

understand v., comprender, entender *kohm-prehn-dehr'*, *ehn-tehn-dehr'* [10]

underwear, ropa interior *roh'-pah een-teh-ree-yohr'*

undress v., desvestirse *dehs-vehs-teer'-seh*

unequal, desigual *dehs-ee-gwahl'*

unfair, injusto *een-hoo'-stoh*

unfortunate, desafortunado *dehs-ah-fohr-too-nah'-doh*

unhappy, infeliz *een-feh-lees'*

unhealthy, malsano *mahl-sah'-noh*

United States, Estados Unidos *eh-stah'-dohs oo-nee'-dohs*

university, universidad (f) *oo-nee-vehr-see-dahd'*

unless, a menos que *ah meh'-nohs keh*

unlucky, de mala suerte *deh mah'-lah swehr'-teh*

unpack, desempaquetar *dehs-ehm-pah-keh-tahr'*

unpleasant, desagradable *dehs-ah-grah-dah'-bleh*

unsafe, inseguro *een-seh-goo'-roh*

until, hasta *ahs'-tah*

untrue, falso *fahl'-soh*

unusual, raro *rah'-roh*

up, arriba *ah-rree'-bah*

upper, superior *soo-peh-ree-yohr'*

upstairs, arriba *ah-rree'-bah*

urgent, urgente *oor-hehn'-teh*

us, nos *nohs*

use n., uso *oo'-soh* [35]

use v., usar *oo-sahr'*

useful, útil *oo'-teel*

useless, inútil *een-oo'-teel*

usual, usual *oo-soo-wahl'*

vacant, libre *lee'-breh*

vacation, vacaciones (f, pl) *vah-kah-syohn'-ehs*

vaccination, vacuna *vah-koo'-nah*

valuable, valioso *vah-lyoh'-soh*

value n., valor (m) *vah-lohr'*

vanilla, vainilla *vah-ee-nee'-lyah*

variety, variedad (f) *vah-ree-eh-dahd'*
veal, ternera *tehr-neh'-rah*
vegetable, legumbre (m) *leh-goom'-breh*
very, muy *mwee*
vest, chaleco *chah-leh'-koh*
victim, víctima *veek'-tee-mah*
view *n.,* vista *vee'-stah* [39]
village, aldea *ahl-deh'-ah*
vinegar, vinagre *vee-nah'-greh*
visa *n.,* visa *vee'-sah*
visit *n.,* visita *vee-see'-tah*
visit *v.,* visitar *vee-see-tahr'* [101, 103]
voice, voz (f) *vohs*
volcano, volcán (m) *vohl-kahn'*
voyage *n.,* viaje (m) *vyah'-heh*

waist, cintura *seen-too'-rah*
wait *v.,* esperar *eh-speh-rahr'* [12, 47]
waiter, camarero, mozo *kah-mah-reh'-roh, moh'-soh* [59]
waiting room, sala de espera *sah'-lah deh eh-speh'-rah* [87]
waitress, camerera, moza *kah-meh-reh'-rah, moh'-sah* [52]
wake up, despertar, despertarse *dehs-pehr-tahr', dehs-pehr-tahr'-seh* [41]
walk *n.,* paseo *pah-seh'-oh;*
walk *v.,* caminar *kah-mee-nahr'* [102]
wall, pared (f) *pah-rehd'*
wallet, cartera *kahr-teh'-rah*
want *v.,* desear, querer *deh-seh-ahr', keh-rehr'* **I want,** quiero, deseo *kyeh'-roh, deh-seh'-oh*
want, quiero, deseo *kyeh'-roh, deh-seh'-oh*
warm, caliente *kah-lyehn'-teh* [55, 58]
warn, avisar *ah-vee-sahr'*
warning, aviso *ah-vee'-soh*
wash *v.,* lavar *lah-vahr'* [41, 77]
wasp, avispa *ah-vees'-pah*
watch *n.,* reloj (m) *reh-lokh'*

watch *v.*, mirar *mee-rahr'*
water, agua (f) *ah'-gwah* [8, 54, 77]
waterfall, catarata, cascada *kah-tah-rah'-tah, kahs-kah'-dah*
way [manner], manera *mah-neh'-rah*
we, nosotros, nosotras *noh-soh'-trohs, noh-soh'-trahs*
weak, débil *deh'-beel*
wear *v.*, llevar *lyeh-vahr'*
weather, tiempo *tyehm'-poh* [5, 8]
Wednesday, miércoles *myehr'-koh-lehs*
week, semana *seh-mah'-nah* [40]
weigh, pesar *peh-sahr'*
weight, peso *peh'-soh*
welcome *n.*, bienvenida *byehn-veh-nee'-dah*
well, bien *byehn* **well done,** bien hecho *byehn eh'-choh*
well [for water], pozo *poh'-soh*
west, oeste (m) *oh-ehs'-teh*
wet, mojado *moh-hah'-doh*
what *interr.*, ¿qué? *keh* **what else?** ¿qué más? *keh mahs*
wheel, rueda *rweh'-dah*
when, cuándo *kwahn'-doh*
whenever, siempre que *syehm'-preh keh*
where, dónde *dohn-deh* **where is?** ¿dónde está? *dohn'-deh eh-stah'* **where are?** ¿dónde están? *dohn'-deh eh-stahn'*
wherever, dondequiera *dohn-deh-kyeh'-rah*
which *interr.*, ¿cuál? *kwahl*
which *rel.*, que *keh*
while, mientras *myehn'-trahs*
whip *n.*, látigo, azote (m) *lah'-tee-goh, ah-soh'-teh*
white, blanco *blahn'-koh* [70, 71]
who *interr.*, ¿quién? *kyehn*
who *rel.*, quien, que *kyehn, keh*
whole, entero *ehn-teh'-roh*
whom *interr.*, ¿a quién? *ah kyehn*
whose *interr.*, ¿de quién? *deh kyehn*

why *interr.*, ¿por qué? *pohr keh*
wide, ancho *ahn'-choh* [71]
width, anchura *ahn-choo'-rah*
wife, esposa *eh-spoh'-sah*
wild, salvaje *sahl-vah'-heh*
willing, dispuesto *dees-pwehs'-toh*
win *v.*, ganar *gah-nahr'*
wind, viento *vyehn'-toh* [7]
window, ventana *vehn-tah'-nah* [41, 87]
windshield, parabrisas (m) *pah-rah-bree'-sahs* [79]
wine, vino *vee'-noh* [58]　**white wine,** vino blanco *vee'-noh blahn'-koh*　**red wine,** vino tinto *vee'-noh teen'-toh*
wing, ala (f) *ah'-lah*
winter, invierno *een-vyehr'-noh*
wipe, limpiar, secar *leem-pyahr', seh-kahr'* [79]
wise, sabio *sah'-bee-yoh*
wish *n.*, deseo *deh-seh'-oh*
wish *v.*, desear *deh-seh-ahr'*　**I wish,** deseo *deh-seh'-oh*
with, con *kohn*
without, sin *seen*
woman, mujer *moo-hehr'* [10]
wonderful, maravilloso *mah-rah-vee-lyoh'-soh*
wood, madera *mah-deh'-rah;* [firewood], leña *leh'-nyah*
woods, bosque *bohs'-keh*
wool, lana *lah'-nah*
word, palabra *pah-lah'-brah*
work *n.*, trabajo *trah-bah'-hoh*
work *v.*, trabajar *trah-bah-hahr'*
world, mundo *moon'-doh*
worried, preocupado *preh-oh-koo-pah'-doh*
worse, peor *peh-ohr'*
worth, valor *vah-lohr'*
wound [injury], herida *eh-ree'-dah*
wrap *v.*, envolver *ehn-vohl-vehr'* [73]
wrist, muñeca *moo-nyeh'-kah*
wristwatch, reloj de pulsera *reh-lokh' deh pool-seh'-rah*

write, escribir *eh-skree-beer'* [13, 31]
writing, escritura *eh-skree-too'-rah*
wrong, equivocado *eh-kee-voh-kah'-doh* **to be wrong,** no
  tener razón *noh teh-nehr' rah-sohn'* [12]

x ray, rayos-x *rah'-yohs-eh'-kees*

yard, patio *pah'-tyoh*
year, año *ah-nyoh'* [92]
yellow, amarillo *ah-mah-ree'-lyoh* [70]
yes, sí *see*
yesterday, ayer *ah-yehr'*
yet, todavía *toh-dah-vee'-yah*
you, usted *oos-tehd'*
young, joven *hoh'-vehn*
your, su *soo*
yours, suyo *soo'-yoh*

zero, cero *seh'-roh*
zipper, cremallera *kreh-mah-lyeh'-rah*

METRIC CONVERSION TABLES

Weight

1 gramo (gm) = 0.04 ounce
1 kilo (kg) = 2.20 pounds
1 ounce = 28.35 gm.
1 pound = 453.59 gm.

Volume

1 litro = 0.91 dry quart
1 litro = 1.06 liquid quarts
1 pint liquid = 0.47 liter
1 US quart liquid = 0.95 liter
1 US gallon = 3.78 liters

Temperature

Celsius (°C):	−17.8	0	10	20	30	37	37.8	100
Fahrenheit (°F):	0	32	50	68	86	98.6	100	212

12

Why We Make This Generous Offer

As a bonus to buyers of this book, Cortina Academy has arranged this special offer of a FREE Language Record and Lesson. Cortina Academy, the world-famous originator of the phonograph method of language learning, develops and publishes the most thorough and effective complete language courses available today. You have a special opportunity for introduction to these outstanding language materials—and there are several important reasons why you should take advantage of this opportunity *now*:

- Cortina's "learn-by-listening" Method is the *natural* way to learn;

- you learn almost without effort—at your own convenience;

- your rewards will be great—including the many business and travel opportunities available to speakers of foreign languages.

So take advantage of this unusual introductory offer. There is no obligation. Just mail the coupon today for your Free Language Record and Lesson.

Cortina Institute of Languages, Dept. GD-P,

17 Riverside Ave., Westport, CT 06880

- -
(COUPON)

CORTINA INSTITUTE OF LANGUAGES

Dept. GD-P, 17 Riverside Avenue, Westport, CT 06880

Please send me by mail—free of charge—the FREE Language Record and Lesson in the one language checked below; also a free booklet which describes fully the complete Course and Method.

(Please check language record you wish)

☐ Spanish ☐ French ☐ German ☐ Italian ☐ Brazilian-Portuguese
☐ Russian ☐ Japanese ☐ Modern Greek ☐ English (for Spanish- or Portuguese-speaking people)

Name ....

Address ....

City .... State............... Zip Code.........

Offer good only in the U.S.A. and Canada.